COUNTRY WALKS AROUND KENDAL

Mary Welsh & Christine Isherwood

Published by Sigma Leisure – an imprint of
Sigma Press, 1 South Oak Lane, Wilmslow, Cheshire SK9 6AR, England.

British Library Cataloguing in Publication Data
A CIP record for this book is available from the British Library.

ISBN: 1-85058-575-X

Cover illustration: The Kent Estuary, looking from Arnside Knott *(Christine Isherwood)*

Maps and illustrations: Christine Isherwood

Typesetting and design by: Sigma Press, Wilmslow, Cheshire

Printed by: MFP Design and Print

Foreword

It would be an interesting exercise to establish which town in Britain has the highest proportion of walkers and hikers in relation to its total population. Kendal would surely feature high on the list. In every direction from the town, and within a radius of a dozen miles, there is a sort of standing invitation to go for a walk – a network of public footpaths and bridleways second to none.

And what a variety of walking! There are coastal walks, riverside walks, woodland walks, pastoral walks, walks in limestone country, walks on gently rounded hills and, of course, walks on rugged Lake District fells. The Kendalian walker is indeed privileged to have such a choice of surfaces on which to place his booted feet and such a choice of scenery to savour.

This excellent book captures the wide ranging types of walks available close to Kendal. It is the ideal companion for walkers who wish to have an authentic experience of this richly varied and beautiful area. Mary Welsh is a true lover of the country-side, and her obvious enjoyment of its sights and sounds will infect the reader. Her awareness of the cry of the curlew, the murmur of the trees, and the breath of the flowers will rub off onto the book's user.

Every chapter in the book enables the walker to enjoy panoramic views. However, as a general rule, the higher one walks, the better the view – and it is on the hilltops too where the walker can feel he has the world at his feet, and that he is, in the words of the Psalmist, "little lower than the angels".

Alan Winstanley LL.B, Clerk & Chief Executive to South Lakeland District Council

Contents

The Kendal coat of arms

Introduction

The hub from which all these walks radiate is the bustling town of Kendal. Its real name is Kirkbie Kendal, which means that it was a village with a church, situated in a dale through which flows the River Kent, the Kent dale.

The Kent is relatively short, rising in Hall Cove below High Street at the head of the Kentmere valley. It is soon joined by feeder streams descending from the slopes of Kentmere Pike, Shipman Knotts, Ill Bell and Froswick. The river, seen on many of these walks, flows through Staveley and on to be joined by the Gowan, Sprint and Mint. After several loops beyond Kendal, the river is swelled by the Gilpin and Bela before it empties into the sea at Morecambe Bay. The river was once navigable to the port at Milnthorpe, six and a half miles from Kendal.

The Auld Grey Town, known as such because of its fine limestone buildings, developed its wealth from the wool of sheep and its many fast-flowing streams. The latter were harnessed to power mills which manufactured cloth from the wool. In the Kent valley grew dyer's broom. This dyed cloth yellow.

It was then redyed with woad (a blue dye) and Kendal green was created. In 1331 Flemish weaver came to Kendal and set up a woollen-weaving industry.

The coat of arms of Kendal, seen over the doorway of the Town Hall, shows tenterhooks for stretching the wool and teasels, seed heads used for bringing up the nap, or pile, on the cloth. Look for the motto 'Pannus mihi panis', meaning wool is my bread.

Kendal lies just outside the high peaks of the Lake District, at the foot of gently rounded hills, through which many of these walks pass. It is often described as the gateway to the Lakes from the south.

Many visitors hurry through the busy town without realising its delights or the delectable walking country easily reached from it.

The walks range from four to ten miles in length. Many of them pass through rolling countryside, passing from pasture to pasture by a variety of stiles and gates. Sometimes these are waymarked; sometimes footpaths and tracks are signposted, sometimes not. This has made it necessary for the author to include, in some walks, detailed instructions. Though this can result in tedious passages, the walks themselves are far from tedious. In fact all of them are a delight to tread.

All routes are on rights of way and these are to be found on the maps itemised for each walk. Ordnance Survey Pathfinder and Outdoor Leisure maps show walls and fences, woodlands and copses and indicate where the footpath goes. Take the relevant map with you and develop map skills, a rewarding activity. Carry your map in a waterproof case.

Most walks are over farmland and low lying hills, but you should carry the gear that you would take for the walks over the tops because the weather can change. Take good waterproofs, an extra sweater, food and drink and some high energy sweets. For all the walks sturdy footwear is essential. In winter take a torch in case your timing is at fault. Carry a whistle.

Key to Maps

All maps are at a scale of 1:50,000 except where otherwise stated.

Motorway or dual carriageway
Major road
Minor road or walled track
Unwalled track
Footpath used in walk
Other footpaths
Railway line + station
Stream, river
Waterfall
Bridge
Building
Church
Built-up area
Deciduous woodland
Coniferous woodland
Parkland
Lake, tarn, etc.
Crags
Scree
Quarry
Limestone pavement
Sand, mud
Marsh, saltmarsh
Parking place

Walking is a wonderful pastime. This book takes you to many of the lovely corners around Kendal. There are many more waiting to be explored. Enjoy your walks. 'Read' the countryside as you go. Look out for wet areas as you begin to learn about the plants that thrive in pools and mosses. Listen for bird-song and then look for the bird in the direction of the call. Look for gate stoops with holes, the origin of the name five-barred gate. Look for slabs of slate with one hole, used as a hinge. See how many types of kissing gates and unusual stiles abound in this lovely area.

Good walking!

1. Grayrigg

Grayrigg – Sunny Bank farm – Simgill farm – Grayrigg Foot farm – Bye Mill – Grayrigg.

Start/Finish: There is limited parking in front of Grayrigg primary school, just before (to the west of) the church (GR 579972). Grayrigg lies 5 miles from Kendal on the A658 Appleby Road.

Type of Walk: This pleasing 6-miler takes you through delightful rolling pastures and alongside quiet gills, generally following the Dales Way and presenting fine views of the Lakeland mountains.

Map: OS Outdoor Leisure 7, The English Lakes, South Eastern area

---

The Walk

The small linear village of Grayrigg sits below Whinfell Beacon. Its three dozen houses gather snugly around the church of St John the Evangelist, which was built in 1837-8. It has a fine crenellated tower, rebuilt after the walls collapsed in 1869. The low roof and square shape make the church seem friendly and welcoming. While in the village look for the row of attractive almshouses erected and endowed by John and Mary Rowlandson, of Ghyll Bank, Grayrigg, in 1869. Opposite the church is

Grayrigg

the Coronation Hall, built to commemorate the coronation of George V in 1911.

Stride east out of the village and take the signposted steps beyond the last house on the right. Walk the narrow footpath and then continue ahead, but look back to enjoy the view of the village. Go on along a hedged track to pass in front of Sunny Bank farm. Grayrigg Quakers met here in the 17th century. In 1696 they built a meeting house and a school at nearby Beck-houses.

Keep to the right of the last barn. Follow the track as it winds slightly right. Pass through a gate into pasture, with the extensive slopes of Grayrigg Forest, no longer tree clad, to the left. Continue on, with a hedge to your right. Just before a large dwelling named Hyning, take the waymarked gate ahead (passing to the right of the house) ignoring the gate on the right.

Climb uphill towards a copse, keeping to the left of the trees,

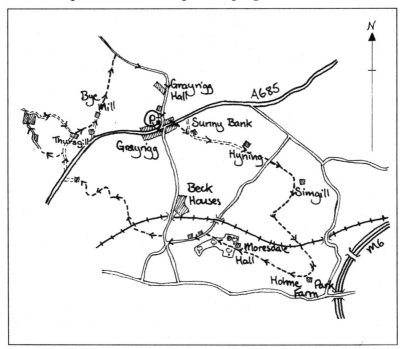

The Howgills

to a gate to a sunken road. Cross and stroll on to the top of the slope and a breathtaking view of the Howgills. The humpy shapes of these fells, like the backs of elephants, stretch along the horizon. The land was taken from Westmorland and given to Yorkshire by Henry VIII.

Descend towards Simgill farm. Pass through a gate towards the farmyard and take another immediately on your right, clearly waymarked. Dawdle along the edge of the pretty gill and continue on a grassy farm track. Where it divides, take the upper way as it swings right across the pasture to a waymarked post. Carry on, slightly to the left, to a good stile that leads into a wet area with birdwatching hides. Leave by the waymarked fence opposite.

Ascend the slope and pass through a gateless gap on your left. Bear diagonally left to the lower of the two gates. Step across the farm track beyond, and head over the grass to cross, with care, the mainline railway track, climbing large white wooden stiles. Go over the footbridge across a tiny beck. Continue ahead, bearing slightly left towards Holme Park farm. Take a stile over a wire fence, to join the Dales Way, where you turn right.

The Dales Way runs from Ilkley to Bowness-on-Windermere, a distance of 84 miles (135km). It was devised in 1968 by Colin Speakman and Tom Willock, members of the West Riding area of the Ramblers Association. It is a route that enables walkers to stroll beside the rivers Wharfe, Dee and Lune. It was first walked in 1969 by Venture Scouts from Bradford Grammar School.

From now on the well stiled, gated and waymarked route is easy to follow. There is another pleasing view over the pasture, to your right, of Grayrigg village. As you approach Morsedale Hall, look out for the waymarks as you cross the bridge over a small beck. Bear right and then immediately left up a narrow path. Cross the tarmacked drive, and then the access drive that leads to the main door of the hall. Take another narrow path through rhododendrons to a kissing gate. Beyond, continue ahead, cross a small stream and take a stone stepped stile to a narrow lane. Turn left and dawdle to the T-junction, where you walk right. Take the signposted gate on the left, opposite a white-painted cottage. Ahead you can look across the gentle countryside into Longsleddale and also, further to the left, the Kentmere valley.

Head on beside the hedge to your left and then descend steadily to cross the railway again by more white stiles. Carry on to the side of a meandering beck (the waymark is on a tree), and continue to a gate. Do not go through but walk left, along the hedge, to pass through a gate on the right to join a track. Go through Green Head farm to stride a metalled track, which bears left. At the bottom of the slope, and before a beck and a cattle grid, look for the difficult-to-see waymark (on the left), directing you right above the stream.

Pass through a gate and cross the footbridge over the beck and continue, left, through Grayrigg Foot farm to the road. Turn right and, within a hundred yards, cross to walk a waymarked track signposted Thursgill. Once over the beck, turn left and climb the slope to a stile, where two hedges meet. Continue on with the hedge to the left. From here you can see, across the fields, a large white house – Shaw End.

Ignore the next waymarked gate because it is here that you leave the Dales Way. Walk on along the track to pass between the hedge and a barn. Follow the track round, first left and then right, and then turn left to pass between farm buildings, with the slurry tank to your right. Pass the farmhouse on your left and at the corner take the track that leads off right.

Stride ahead and pass through two gates. Bear left to walk with a wall and a hedge to the left. Go through the next gate and then another, immediately on the left. Cut across the corner to a gate to a track which passes in front of a bungalow and comes to Thursgill farm. From this point you can see where you walked a mile back. The detour round the hill keeps you on the right of way.

Turn left just before the farmhouse and pass through the yard. (Knock on the farmhouse door for instructions if the bull is present.) Then continue on a grassy track that descends quite steeply to the side of the fast-flowing beck. Go on upstream towards Bye Mill, once a cornmill, where you cross the footbridge over the stream.

Turn left and walk past the dwelling to cross a second footbridge. Continue beside the beck and then climb above the trees and carry on to the road. Walk right and, as you go, look through the hedge to glimpse the tower of Grayrigg church. Cross the low-arched bridge over Grayrigg Hall Beck and then walk past Grayrigg Hall farm to return to the village. The Hall is the site for the agricultural show held in September. The original hall, which stood further away from the village, fell into disrepair and was demolished in the 18th century.

Walk right to rejoin your car.

2. Brigflatts to Firbank Fell

Brigflatts – High Oaks – Lincoln's Inn Bridge – Firbank Fell –
St Gregory's Church – Brigflatts.

Start/Finish: Large layby on the A683 opposite the narrow lane
which leads to Brigflatts (GR 641913), 6 miles from Kendal.

Type of Walk: This 7½-mile walk takes you on the same journey
as George Fox, the Quaker, made, along rights of way, from the
Meeting House to Firbank Fell. It comes close to the lovely River
Lune and, using the Dales Way, it passes through delectable
countryside west of Sedbergh.

Map: OS Pathfinder 617 Sedbergh and Baugh Fell.

The Walk

Stroll the lane opposite the layby, which leads to Brigflatts, once
a settlement of flax-weavers. Pass the Quaker burial ground,
and then, on the left, the old meeting house.

Brigflatts Meeting House

At Whitsun 1652, George Fox preached under a yew tree in Sedbergh's parish churchyard. He would not go inside because he believed a church was 'a fellowship of God's people', not a building. He then stayed at Brigflatts, which has a Quaker Meeting House built in 1675.

From Brigflatts he walked to Firbank Fell and preached, perched on top of a rock now known as Fox's Pulpit, to over a thousand Seekers, people who were seeking a new form of Christian worship.

Go inside and enjoy the peace of the simple white-washed room, with its wooden gallery and bench seats surrounding a plain table. Look for the en-closed area, between the door and the gallery, where Friends left their sheepdogs during meet-ings. Sit in the garden, a mass of snowdrops, in early spring. From here there is a good view of Brigflatts farm where Fox stayed the night on his journey. He attended a meeting at Borrett, a large farm nearby, owned by the Benson family, who were persecuted for their be-liefs.

Snowdrops

Return to the end of the lane, turn left and, with care, walk along the A-road for just over half a mile. Look right, as you go, to see the magnificently restored Ingmire Hall, which in the 1680s was the home of the Catholic Otway family, who had great sympathy for the Quakers.

Take the footpath, signposted High Oaks, on the right. Walk ahead to cross a clapper bridge over Haverah Beck, bear half-left uphill, and then right before the hedge. Join a signposted hedged track leading left into the attractively restored settlement. Beyond the first house, High Oaks farm (1706), turn right. Ignore the stile on the left and walk the track to a three-armed signposted stile, beyond which you turn right to walk a pasture. Continue on, ignoring the right turn, to walk a gated grassy way, with glorious views of the Howgills ahead.

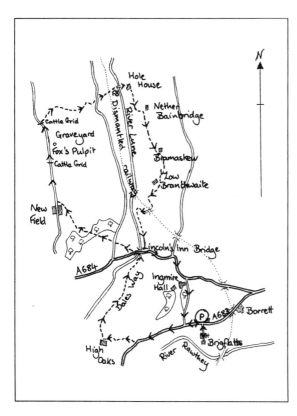

Keep to the right of Luneside farm and follow the waymarks to take a signposted gate on the left for Lincoln's Inn Bridge. Stroll the stiled way and, as it nears the Lune, look for mergansers and dippers. Cross the lovely narrow old road bridge, with care, and take the easy-to-miss stepped, signposted stile in the wall on the right, beyond Lincoln's Inn farm. Stride uphill, with the hedge to the right, to a ladderstile from where there is a very good view of the Lune viaduct. This carried the Ingleton-Tebay line, part of the London North-Western Railway, which was closed to passengers in 1953.

Fox's Pulpit, Firbank Fell

Continue ahead to the next ladderstile onto a lane, which you cross to pass through a gate. Climb up the slope towards a glorious wood, which is edged with lofty beech, bearing left just before the trees. Climb a stile, now on your right, into the woodland, to ascend through sycamore and birch, where the floor is glorious with bluebells in spring. Look for marsh tits high in the branches. Emerge from the trees and climb up the pasture to a wall corner. Bear half-left to a gateless gap. Continue to the next gate and then bear diagonally left to join a farm track to Newfield farm and the narrow road over Firbank Fell. Turn right and stride uphill over the windy moorland. Just beyond the cattle grid, take a ladderstile on the right that gives access to the foot of Fox's Pulpit.

This is a huge, fissured, lichen-clad outcrop of natural rock on the fellside. On a June Sunday morning in 1652, finding the tiny Firbeck Chapel filled to overflowing, the Quaker chose to speak to the great multitude of followers on this lonely hillside. Today there is no trace of the chapel.

Return to the road and walk on to visit the walled graveyard. Continue downhill and just before the next cattle grid take the stile on the right. Stride ahead beside the wall to your right, and then the fence, where it can be wet underfoot. Go on, with a larch plantation now to your right. Climb the stile and continue ahead along a sunken cart track with a delightful gill to your right. Carry on downhill, keeping beside the hedge on your left when the track temporarily disappears. Then pick it up again and follow it to the B6257, which you cross.

Take the metal gate on your right and walk ahead to a wooden gate. Beyond, descend the steep slope, cross the dismantled railway and continue downhill to the fisherman's footbridge over the Lune. Follow the path left to walk beside the surging water and press on where it turns away from the river, beside a small feeder stream. At Hole House, turn right to follow the arrowed way through the buildings at the back of the farm-house. Beyond the gate, turn right to follow the signpost for Nether Bainbridge. Continue beside the fence as it swings left and then the wall, to come to a signposted gate on your right. Go through and stride beside the wall on your left.

At the three-armed signpost, which directs you right of a barn, take a very narrow gap stile on the left and then turn right to walk a pleasing hedged track, right. Go on along the gated way, following the telegraph poles to a stone stepped stile. Stride ahead to the right of Bramaskew farm and go on the stiled way to a painted Dales Way sign, over the pasture, on a gate to your right. Beyond, head along the hedged and walled track. Descend steadily and then aim for a signposted ladderstile to the left of Low Branthwaite, with its splendid bank barn. Once over the stile, turn left, and walk to a four-armed signpost, where you turn right. Continue beside the wall on your left, pass under the dismantled railway and stride on to the side of the Lune once more.

Turn left to walk downstream and follow the stiled way to the east end of Lincoln's Inn Bridge. At the road, turn left and walk with care along the A684.

Visit the disused St Gregory's Church (early 1860s) on your right. St Gregory's is now vested in the Redundant Churches Fund. Enjoy the glorious stained-glass windows made by Frederick George Smith, the glass of which seems almost sculpted.

Construction of the church was due to Miss Frances Upton of Ingmire Hall. When the Ingleton branch of the London and North-Western Railway was built, the company sent a Mr Foyers as scripture reader to the navvies. When time came for the railway builders and Mr Foyers to move on, local people petitioned Miss Upton to make it possible for him to stay. This she did providing him with St Gregory's.

Ignore the footpath by the church and go on along the road to take the signposted track on the right, just beyond the entrance to Ingmire Hall. Keep to the left of the hall's castellated lodge. Stride this pleasing way and continue to the A683. Turn left to rejoin your car.

3. The Helm

The foot of The Helm – St John's View – Middleshaw – The Helm.

Start/Finish: A large layby, the first after the Westmorland General hospital on the east side of the A65, 1 mile from Kendal (GR 528889).

Type of Walk: A delightful 6½ miles through the pleasing countryside, south-east of Kendal. The Helm, a hill of Silurian rock, rises 605 feet, and dominates the route throughout its length.

Map: OS Pathfinder 627 SD 48/58 Milnthorpe.

The Walk

Walk on from the layby for a few yards to turn left into a narrow lane on your left. Take the stile immediately on your right. Walk up a short slope and turn right to join a bridleway to Stang. Continue below The Helm, where the slopes support scattered hawthorn, rowan, oak and gorse. As you go, pause regularly to enjoy the ever extending views of Whitbarrow Scar and the Kent Estuary.

The Helm

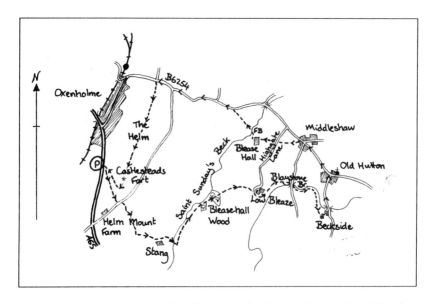

Where the path divides, keep to the lower branch, with the wall to your right. Beyond a gate, continue along a wide hedged and walled cart track. Cross a narrow lane and walk on downhill to Helm Mount farm, with Farleton Fell away to the left. Keep to the left of the two dwellings and take the stone stile tucked away in the near-left corner of the garden of the second house. Walk diagonally left to half-way along the boundary hedge to cross the stream by clapper or tractor bridge. Beyond, climb uphill with the wall to your left to pass an electricity pylon on your right.

Go on to join a very narrow lane, where you turn left. Once over the cattle grid, bear right over a pasture, to a footbridge over Saint Sunday's Beck. Ignore the ladderstile and turn left to walk upstream. The charming beck is shadowed by graceful alders. Here you might see a green woodpecker feeding in the pasture before it returns to Stang Wood. The beck changes its name at Stainton and becomes a feeder for the Lancaster Canal.

On reaching a wire fence, take a stepped stile on the right and, beyond, continue upstream. Carry on the stiled way to enter Bleasehall Wood, which has several massive oaks and

Green woodpecker in pasture

where there has been much replanting with the same species. Emerge from the woodland by a kissing gate and stride on to the ladderstile ahead. To the left is an ornate syphon well, used in supplying water for the canal.

Strike ahead to a stile in the far corner of the wire fence on the right. Once over, continue with the hedge and the wall to your left. Ahead are the Howgills. Go on to Low Blease farm. Pass through the metal farm gate, bear left, then right and follow the track round right and left again. Walk ahead to cross a stream to another metal gate. Stride across a pasture to the side of Peasey Beck. This carries water from Killington reservoir and is added to the Lancaster Canal by a feeder.

Turn left to walk to a reinforced access track. Turn right and continue to Blaystone Bridge, which you cross right. Take the signposted way immediately on your left and walk upstream to a narrow lane. Turn left to step into the hamlet of Beckside. Once there was a cornmill here. Spend some time seeking out the hamlet's picturesque waterfall, a little upstream.

Turn left on the narrow lane and walk into the hamlet of St John's View. Visit the little church beside the school and the village hall. The church was rebuilt in 1873. It possesses a 15th century chalice, which is kept in a bank for safety. Near the church is a house called Church View where John Wesley once slept on his way to Whitehaven from Leeds.

Leave the hamlet by a kissing gate to the left of the hall. Strike diagonally across the school playing field to another kissing gate. Continue in the same general direction to a gate. Beyond, walk uphill with a hedge to your right to a ladderstile. Stride on to pass through a gate onto a metalled track, which you cross to pass through a copse. Take the right of two stiles and head diagonally to the bottom right corner of the pasture onto a lane. Bear left to walk through the pleasing hamlet of Middleshaw.

At the T-junction, cross the road and take the signposted footpath opposite. Beyond the next stile, keep beside the hedge on your right. Pass through the gate on your right and walk uphill by a wall on your right. A stile gives access to the delightful grassy Highgate Lane. Turn left and take a stile almost immediately on your right. Climb straight uphill with the hedge to your left. Drop down the slope, keeping to the right of a bungalow, to join a very narrow lane. Turn left to pass a limekiln and then the picturesque Blease Hall.

Blease Hall

The charming old house was built about 1600 by a merchant who made his money in Kendal, manufacturing cloth. In the attic there is said to be a 'dobbie stone' which is believed to keep the devil at bay.

Follow the lane round right and pass through a red metal gate. Bear right to pass through another gate and continue to a footbridge over Saint Sunday's Beck. Climb straight up the slope to a gate in the top right corner. From here enjoy a glorious retrospective view of the fells about Barbon.

Continue on with the Langdale Pikes ahead and The Helm to your left. Drop toward Strickley farm and join the road by passing through a gap in the hedge and then walking right to a gate. Turn left and, with care, walk the road in the direction of Oxenholme. Go on the steadily climbing way to the Station Inn. The name Oxenholme means a place where oxen came to drink. It became a village and a very busy rail centre with the coming of the main railway to Scotland.

Take the track opposite the inn and, beyond the cattle grid, ascend a grassy way, on your left, which climbs relentlessly to the triangulation point on The Helm. From this grand summit you have a 360 degrees view of the surrounding mountains and the estuary – and where you have parked. It is believed that this was the site of Castlesteads fort, built by the Romans for a look-out while they were building their fort at Watercrook.

Go on from the summit and descend. Follow a grassy track right and continue downhill to the layby to rejoin your car.

4. Dent

Dent Town – Flinter Gill – South Lord's Land – River Dee and the Dales Way – Dent Town.

Start/Finish: The extensive National Park car park at the north-west end of Dent Town, 11 miles from Kendal (GR 704873). Take the A684 Kendal to Sedbergh and then drive on through narrow lanes to Dent Town.

Type of Walk: A superb 6-mile walk through remote, peaceful Dentdale, where green pastures cradle the River Dee. The climb through Flinter Gill is a delight, though steep for most of the way. The beck tumbles in many noisy cascades beside the track and there are glorious views over the dale through the trees.

Map: OS Outdoor Leisure 2 Yorkshire Dales, Western area

The Walk

Dent Town, as the village is often called to distinguish it from the dale, lies in Cumbria but is within the Yorkshire Dales National Park. It stands on ground above the River Dee and is shadowed by the steep slopes of Middleton Fell, Rise Hill, Whernside and Barbon High Fell. It is noted for its 'terrible knitters', its cobbled streets, its famous son and its church built on 11th century foundations.

From the car park cross the main street and walk ahead up a narrow lane, signed To The Shop on the Green, between pleasing cottages. Pass the village green, where children play on swings and slides. Continue, following an even narrower lane signposted Flinter Gill, to join a steep, rough, gated bridleway. It was once a popular packhorse route from Dent to the port of Lancaster.

To the left the beck descends in noisy, white-topped falls, having gathered its waters on the slopes of Great Coum. Oak trees edge the way and host innumerable small birds. Look for

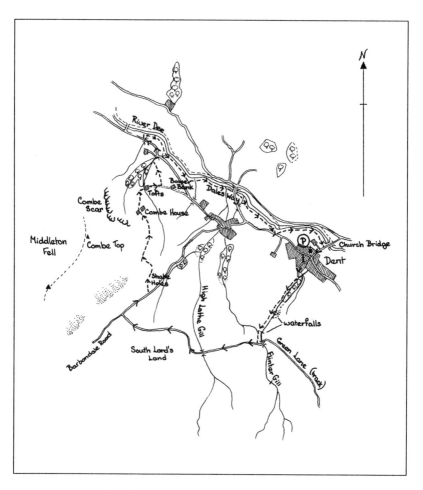

tree creepers, climbing the fissured bark, mouse-like birds with white fronts. In spring the sweet songs of small migrants ease the climb and in summer the way is bordered with cranesbill, bellflowers and sweet cicely.

Continue climbing. Soon the track passes out of the trees and the impetuous beck is seen as a quiet mountain stream dawdling through undulating moorland. In winter the scattered ash and rowan about the grassy slopes, beyond the wall, play host to dozens of noisy fieldfares and redwings.

Meadow Cranesbill and Bellflower

Just before the last gate over the track, a well placed seat enables you comfortably to enjoy glorious Dentdale. Beyond the gate, walk on to the signposted Green Lane, an ancient highway which links Barbondale with Deepdale and was used by coal miners and quarrymen who worked on the nearby fells. Turn right. Enjoy this high-level way from where there are more superb views over pastures to the Howgills; if these are dusted with snow then the view is even more spectacular. The easy way continues below South Lord's Land, which lies below the austere slopes of Towns Fell. The wide-walled track crosses the narrow High Lathe Gill by a deep-sided bridge. Ahead loom the steep grass and scree slopes of Middleton Fell.

Where the track joins the quiet Barbondale Road, turn right to stride for 500 yards. Take the signposted left turn to walk a wide grassy way, passing below Stone Rigg and beside shake holes. These are sometimes called swallow holes (where rainwater is swallowed). The surface once concentrated the rainfall so that it collected in a wide hollow. In time chasms formed below, allowing blocks of rock to fall in and so leave the hollow.

Flinter Gill in winter-time

At the boundary wall ahead, climb the ladderstile to your left. Keep beside the wall on your left to quickly join a good track. Follow this delightful way as it gradually bears right and continues as a wide grassy shelf, along the same contour, below the steep scree slopes of Combe Top. Stroll on this lovely remote way to come to Combe House – now derelict but once a fine small dwelling. It stands below the even steeper slopes of Combe Scar.

Walk round the back of the house and bear right to follow the grassy track downhill. Follow it as it swings left to pass through a gap in the derelict wall. Go on descending to pass through another gap. The track then leads to a ford. Left of this, in a hidden gill, is a small slate footbridge over the narrow stream. Cross this and walk left for a few yards and then climb straight up the bank. Walk ahead between Toft farmhouse and its outbuildings to its access track, which you descend. When Bower Bank comes into view, look for the waymarked gate on the left. Beyond the gate, drop gently, and diagonally, to the bottom left corner of the pasture. Go on along a tarmacked zig-zag to pass a dwelling to join a narrow road.

Turn left and follow the road as it swings sharply right to come nearer to the River Dee. Go on for 400 yards to come to a signposted stile. It directs you right towards the bank of the river, using the stiled and waymarked Dales Way, which takes you easily back to Dent.

Don't miss the steps down to the riverbank. Look out for several pairs of dippers that frequent the shallows of the river. As you approach Barth Bridge, notice the flood holes needed when the river is overfull. As you near Dent, with its houses gathered tightly around its lovely church, walk carefully along a 50-yard stretch of the road. Then continue along the river bank until you reach Church Bridge, just north-east of the village.

Turn right to walk through the narrow streets where, in the absence of pavements, the cobbles stretch from doorway to doorway. Once galleries jutted overhead, making the streets appear even narrower and it was on these that the 'terrible knitters' often sat. Men, women and children knitted at home and on their way to the fields to work to supplement their meagre incomes. According to legend, their needles became red-hot and they had to pause to let them cool!

In the centre of the village, look for the large slab of Shap granite, now a drinking fountain, a memorial to Adam Sedgwick, the pioneer geologist. He was born in Dent in 1785, the son of the vicar. A paved way leads from behind the fountain to the church, which has several memorials to the Sedgwicks. St Andrew's, a large church for such a little village, was rebuilt in 1417 and it has a splendid three-deck pulpit.

Adam Sedgwick's Memorial

5. Tosca

A65 – Tosca – Old Town – Mansergh – Belle Vue – A65

Start/Finish: A layby on the north side of the A65 beside a prominent footpath sign for Tosca, three and a half miles from junction 36 on the M6. The layby is just beyond Spittal farm, where the A-road makes a sharp curve. It lies ten miles from Kendal (GR 583800).

Type of Walk: This six-and-a-half-mile walk takes you through the lovely, rolling, wooded countryside west of Kirkby Lonsdale and south-east of Kendal. It is easy walking all the way and you will rarely meet another person. It is one of the quietest walks in this book, with no traffic noise to intrude on your solitary wandering.

Map: OS Pathfinder 627 SD48/58 Milnthorpe.

The Walk

The A65 is known as the longest country lane in England. It starts in Kendal and continues all the way to Leeds. Ten miles from Kendal the footpath sign Tosca intrigues many motorists. This walk sets out to find this unusually named place and to enjoy the delightful surrounding countryside.

From the layby walk the wide access track towards Fleet farm, as directed by the signpost. Go through the outbuildings and pass through double gates to stride the continuing track. Go ahead through the pastures, bearing to the left of Lowther Plantation, to a three-armed bridleway signpost. (At the time of writing the fourth arm, the one you need to follow, stood forlornly against the wall).

Pass through a gate north of the signpost (ahead in the same direction), and cross the pasture to the far left corner, to come to the side of the chattering Lupton Beck. Beyond the stream lies Hungerhills Plantation. Stroll on the pleasing way, through

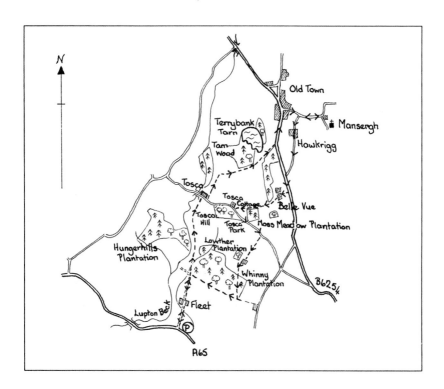

Grey wagtails

a huge pasture, keeping parallel with the beck, which is edged with alder and oak. Skirt Tosca Hill, a gentle mound of just under 500 feet, and drop gently to a signposted gate to a narrow lane.

Opposite stands Tosca, a fine house which was once three cottages. In 1231 it is recorded as Toskerth and the Records Office has a mention of an Adam de Toskbek living there in 1339. To the left, along the lane, is a pleasing stone bridge over Lupton Beck. The pretty stream is the haunt of dippers, grey wagtails, woodpeckers and long tailed tits.

From the gate to the lane, turn right and, after a few yards, take the gate, signposted Old Town, on the left. Stride the clear track beyond, to pass through a waymarked gate. Take the waymarked gate, immediately on your right and walk left, uphill to pass through the next gate. Turn right and walk beside a wall, and then a hedge, to your right. Climb the stile in the right corner. Saunter on with Tarn Wood to your left and walled

Tosca

undulating pastures to your right. Go slowly here and enjoy the quiet remoteness.

Take the next stile, a ladder with three rungs. The rungs have large gaps between them, and strong arms or long legs are needed to climb them. Bear half left to pass Terrybank Tarn, a blue sheet of reed-fringed water, shadowed by willows. Legend suggests that it is very deep and that one day an attempt was made to drive a carriage and horses through it. Neither the carriage nor the horses emerged on the other side.

Go through the waymarked gate into a pasture and walk up the side of woodland that now lies to your right. Climb steadily to a signposted stone stile to the B6254, where you turn left to walk into Old Town. Look right for a dramatic view of Barbon Low Fell and Middleton Fell, with Barbondale 'creeping' between the two. You also have a fine view of Mansergh church.

The tiny hamlet of Old Town consists of a few attractive houses. One large building, now three or more dwellings, has a datestone with EC 1542-1910 on it; the Conder family inhabited the house for 368 years. Continue to the end of the hamlet. Look here, on the right, to see an old milestone which tells you that it is three miles to Kirkby Lonsdale, nine to Kendal and 253 to London.

Return to the narrow lane, now on your left, to walk down the hedged way for half a mile, to visit the church of St Peter, Mansergh, seen earlier. At the foot of the track, leading right to the church gate, is Rigmaden school, built in 1839 and now used as a village hall. St Peter's was built in 1880 on the site of an earlier church. It stands on glorious high ground overlooking the gentle rolling countryside through which the walk continues.

Go back along the narrow lane to turn left into the access track (not waymarked) to Hawkrigg farm. From here look across to see St Peter's again and then beyond towards the village of Barbon. It snuggles at the foot of Barbondale, its church's square tower very plain to see. Go through the farmyard and pass

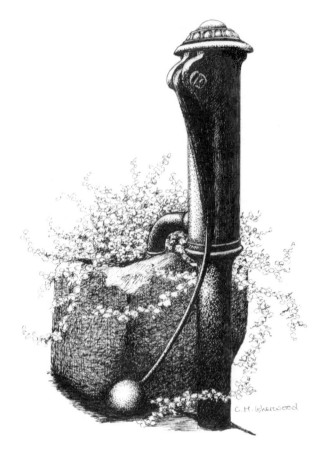

Pump at Old Town

through a double gate and walk on. Take the right of two gates, waymarked, to walk a pleasant grassy way between hedges, to come to the B6254.

Turn left and descend gently to take a right turn, signposted bridleway to Tosca Cottage. Walk towards Belle Vue farmhouse and bear right round the side of the stone barn. Continue behind the farm buildings, following a track. At the hedge, turn right and walk on to a gate.

Continue on beside the plantation on your right. Beyond the trees, stride ahead along the gated way, keeping beside the wall on your left. Pass the west side of Moss Meadow Plantation, on your left, and then head across the pasture to a signposted gate to the road. Tosca Cottage lies to your right. Turn left and walk the quiet lane with, to your right, Tosca Park woodland, re-planted in 1953.

Stroll on to pass the south side of Moss Meadow Plantation, passed earlier. At the end of the trees, walk a short distance to leave the lane by an unwaymarked gate on the right, at the point where the road begins to descend (600 yards from the gate close to Tosca Cottage).

Walk ahead from the gate, keeping beside the wall on the left and heading towards a fine-looking barn, which soon comes into view. Pass behind the barn and then continue on beside a wire fence to your right. Pass through the tall metal gate into Whinny Plantation, which was planted in 1961, and follow the glorious path through the trees to join a reinforced track. Turn left and stroll the pleasing way to emerge from the trees by another tall metal gate.

Turn sharp right, to pass through another gate to walk the south side of the woodland. Cross a tiny stream, where conven-ient, and climb steadily uphill. A short descent brings you to the track from Fleet farm, taken earlier. Turn left to retrace your steps through the farmyard and on to the layby on the A65.

6. Hutton Roof

Crooklands roundabout – Aikbank – Newbiggin Crags –
Hutton Roof – Lupton – Aikbank – roundabout.

Start/Finish: A layby on the left, 100 yards along the A65,
south-east of Crooklands roundabout (GR 536825), 5 miles from
the centre of Kendal.

Type of Walk: A glorious 8-mile walk through grand countryside
and over magic upland areas of limestone scars and pavements.
Among the boulders, clints and grykes that so adorn this pleasing
area thrive the typical bushes, trees and other plants of limestone
soil.

Map: OS Pathfinders 627 48/58 Milnthorpe. 637 56/57 Burton-
in-Kendal

Farleton Knott (Lancaster Canal in foreground)

The Walk

From the layby, cross the road with care and walk on 50 yards to another layby, which you leave by a signposted stile. Stride ahead, beside the hedge on your right, over two pastures to Dove House farm, where you turn right. At the T-junction stride left, with Farleton Knott to your right. This was once a beacon hill and a very important link in a chain of defences which warned of marauding Scots and of a possible Spanish landing. It is the grand landmark seen close to Junction 36 on the M6.

Continue along the quiet lane to cross Nook Bridge over Lupton Beck. Take the gate on the left, signposted Aikbank. Press on with the hedge to your left. Follow the tractor route, which climbs a slope on the right. The way continues above the

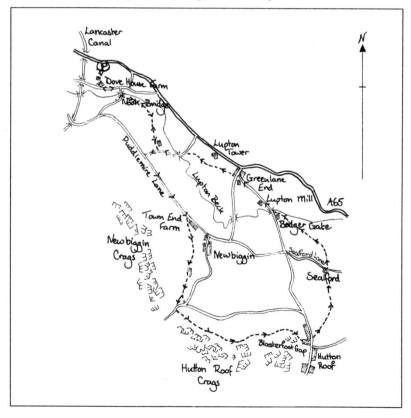

fenced wooded slopes that drop steeply down to the hurrying stream. Where the fence begins to descend towards the beck, stride right across the pasture to a stile. Beyond go on with the hedge to your left to climb the next stile. Then drop down the slope to pass through three gates, to the right of Aikbank, to join a narrow lane where you turn right.

Walk 200 yards, then bear left along the delightfully named Puddlemire Lane. This gated way runs below the austere slopes of Farleton Fell, with Puddle Mire to the left, both covered in gorse ablaze with sweet smelling blossom. Enjoy the pleasing views across the rolling pastures to the foot of Ingleborough.

Turn right immediately before the first dwelling and take a short walled track. Beyond the gate, bear left to climb steadily the limestone skirts of Newbiggin Crags. At a large post, turn right and ascend for another 200 yards to take a good grassy track on your left. Keep above the limestone wall and continue along the delightful way to pass through a gate to a narrow lane, which you cross. Climb the ladder stile to follow the clear path over Hutton Roof Crags.

The crags support many colourful flowering plants. The turf

Ingleborough from the top of Hutton Roof

is kept short by grazing sheep, which stop the growth of trees and shrubs that would shade out the flowers. Look for extensive stands of juniper, the prickly foliage of which deters hungry sheep. Crush some narrow leaves and enjoy the aroma. The berries, loved by coal tits, are used to flavour gin.

Saunter on in an easterly direction, enjoying the spectacular views and the attractive terrain, through holly, rowan and juniper. Stroll the continuing ridge, with extensive valleys to the right and the left. The carboniferous limestone you see about you was formed 300 million years ago from the remains of minute animals and plants that collected on the floor of a warm shallow sea. Earth movements brought the limestone to the surface and an ancient glacier exposed the limestone to weathering by rainwater.

Follow the main track as it begins its pleasing descent through magnificent limestone pavement to the village of Hutton Roof. Walk left towards the post office. Make time to visit the small but beautiful church of St John. It lies next to the old school. The church is built of sandstone, quarried close to the village.

Take the footpath on the right, just beyond the post office, signposted Sealford. Stride the hedged track and then continue ahead on the stiled way over six pastures. Some of the stiles are double; they are easy to spot and the route, unwaymarked, continues in the same direction as the pylons that march along to your right. Keep to the right of the houses at Sealford to join Sealford Lane, where you turn left.

Look for the well restored stile on your right, 50 yards up the lane, almost obscured by a huge sycamore. Beyond, head left over the huge pasture to a stile in the far corner. The next stile, a double one, is half way along the hedge. Beyond, head over another large pasture. The wet area here is a favourite haunt of oyster catchers. They plunge their long, stout orange-red bills into the ooze after worms.

Keep to the right of Badger Gate (1781). Join the road by a

stile and cross Lupton Beck by a sturdy bridge. Proceed along the hedged lane to pass Lupton Mill, now a private dwelling with the millstones in its garden. Press on to Greenlane End, where at the sharp bend turn left.

A narrow stile on the right, beyond the houses on the right, gives access to more quiet pastures. Walk ahead to the gap stile in the boundary hedge. Beyond, you have a good view of the crenellated Lupton Tower, once a farmhouse with a folly; now a vegetarian restaurant and hotel. Stride slightly left to a stile, over the next fence and then walk on with a small stream to your right. Where the stream goes underground, take a large black gate on your left to continue in the same general direction. Keep by the fence on your right to climb a stile below in a hollow.

Wild daffodils

Strike across the next field, keeping to the left of a ruined building and then tread carefully, if you are walking in spring, through a vast carpet of daffodils to a wooden footbridge over the Lupton Beck. Cross and continue on along a rough track that brings you back to Aikbank. From here retrace your outward route via Nook Bridge and Dove House farm to rejoin your car.

7. Lancaster Canal and the River Kent

Kendal — Sedgwick — River Kent — Kendal

Start/Finish: Centre of Kendal

Type of Walk: Easy walking all the way. This 8-mile route takes you along part of the towpath of the Lancaster Canal which, alas, no longer has water. It returns you through the delectable countryside about the River Kent.

Map: OS Landranger 97, Kendal to Morecambe

The Walk

In the 18th century the roads in the north of England were very poor. Coal, essential for the emergent industries, came into the county by sea and the Lancaster Canal was constructed so that it could then be transported easily and cheaply to its destination. Limestone, abundant in the north, was much needed for agricultural land in the south, and the empty boats could carry it after they had discharged their coal. The canal was opened on June 18, 1819 and was soon nicknamed the black and white canal.

Leave Kendal Town Hall by Lowther Street, cross Miller Bridge and continue along Aynham Road to take the turning on the left, Queen Katharine Street. This leads to the site of the canal where you turn right. The waterway was designed by John Rennie, and was in use until 1938. Sadly this stretch was filled in 1955, but the route has been preserved by constructing a cycle way along the cut.

To the left, on a huge glacial mound, stands all that remains of Kendal Castle. To visit, leave by the canal bridge ahead and walk up Sunnyside to a footpath that ascends the mound to the ruins. A wide grassed track edges the dry moat and leads to a gate by which you can enter the grassy area within the ruined wall.

Kendal Castle

The original entrance was probably by a drawbridge and a portcullis. The castle was built by an early Baron of Kendal, possibly Gilbert Fitz Reinfreed, sheriff of Lancaster, between 1205 and 1215. Katharine Parr, the surviving wife of Henry VIII, spent a very happy childhood there. The castle was acquired by the town and opened to the public to mark Queen Victoria's diamond jubilee in 1896.

Return by the same route to continue along the old cut. Cross the road ahead and continue on the well signposted cycle way.

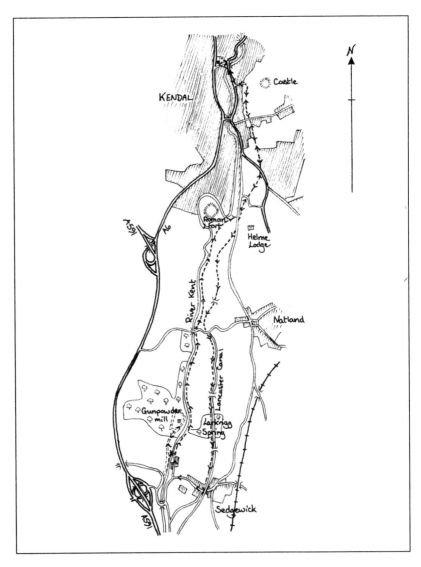

Pass below the cobbled Kendal Change or Changeline Bridge, which enabled canal horses to pass to the towpath on the opposite bank. Beyond, look right across fields to a mock Tudor house, built in the style of the Netherfield Toll House, which stood on the site. In icy weather, water was released from this

The River Kent

stretch of the canal to flood a field for skating. Now the houses built on the field form the Rinkfield Estate.

Pass below the next bridge and go on beneath a row of magnificent beeches. Here a signboard says that you are 14 miles from Tewitfield, the terminus of the cruising section of the canal, and 1 mile from Kendal.

Cross Natland Road and walk on for 100 yards to take a gate on the right to join a footpath, once the towpath. As you continue, look for the grassy bed of the waterway, which can be seen intermittently. Stride the stiled way and enjoy the pleasing countryside all around. Go on beside the old water channel, passing below Natland Hall Bridge, Crow Park Bridge and then Larkrigg Hall Bridge. Continue through the delightful deciduous woodland of Larkhall Spring, with the bed of the waterway to your left. Beyond, carry on the waymarked path to the forlorn Horse Park Bridge, 'stranded' in the middle of the pasture with no trace of the canal.

Beyond, the path leads to an iron gate and the old wharf where coal was unloaded. Here the bed is now used for garden extensions and as a builder's yard. Then a well buttressed skew aqueduct is reached. Descend the sturdy steps to the attractive village of Sedgwick. It has many pleasant cottages gathered around the post office. These were built originally for estate and other workers by the Wakefield family, who brought the gunpowder industry to Sedgwick in the latter part of the 18th century.

Stroll on along the road to pass Sedgwick house, built in 1869, and continue to the side of the River Kent, where you turn right. Walk the signposted bridleway until you reach the portalled suspension bridge. Cross, and turn right, to walk through woodland to see ruins of the gunpowder works. There are more ruins by the Caravan Club and it is well worth asking permission to view this industrial archaeology. John Wakefield sited his works here because there was a plentiful supply of alder, birch and juniper for charcoal and water power provided by the fast flowing Kent.

Return across the bridge and continue upstream. Look right to see the Sedgwick drumlins – more glacial mounds. Look out for the stile where the riverside footpath leaves the bridleway

Goosanders at Watercrook

and stroll on the lovely way. Continue to Hawes Bridge from where there is a dramatic view of the raging force below.

Do not cross the bridge but walk on, upstream, to take a footpath signposted Kendal, on your left. Stroll the stiled way, continuing beside the river where it makes a small meander. Then the path heads toward the road. Pause here and look over a wall to see the huge crook of the river, enfolding two fields. On these, within this enormous curve, Watercrook, was sited Kendal's Roman fort, Alavna. Various artefacts have been found and these can be seen in the Kendal museum.

Go on to the road. Turn right and walk to cross Natland Road, taken earlier. Join the cycleway, the old towpath, to return to the centre of Kendal.

8. Warton Crag

Warton – Warton Crag – Crag Foot – Leighton Park – Warton

Start/Finish: Car park in old quarry, north side of Crag Road, Warton, (GR 496724), 13 miles from Kendal.

Type of Walk: This delightful 5½-mile walk takes you to Warton Crag from where you enjoy the magnificent view. It continues through acres of deciduous trees and returns through a nature reserve. Clear tracks and paths for most of the way. Steady climb to the Crag but the going is easier after that.

Map: OS Pathfinder 636 SD 37/47 Grange-over-Sands

The Walk

In the north western corner of Lancashire lie small limestone hills, tiny valleys, reclaimed mosslands and a wealth of woodland. One of the highest hills is Warton Crag, its series of stepped scars overshadowing the linear village of Warton.

Leave the parking area, turn left at the lane and then right along Main Street to visit the church of St Oswald. Here on

Blackthorn and Yew – both grow on Warton Crag

July 4 the church flies the stars and stripes. In 1983 the flag was first flown to mark the two hundredth anniversary of the ending of the American War of Independence. The link between the flag and the village is that the first American president, George Washington, could, tenuously, trace his roots back to Warton. The 15th century tower of the church was built by an ancestor, Robert Washington. Look for the Washington coat of arms, mullets and bars – the stars and stripes – on the outside wall.

Walk back along Main Street and notice on the right side the sturdy Washington House. Though rebuilt in the 18th century, it has a datestone of 1612. Continue along the street, which has many attractive old houses. Turn left into Coach Road to begin a steady climb. Continue to just beyond the last house and take a bridleway, signposted Crag Foot, which leads into deciduous woodland.

Ignore the permissive path on the left – this is the return route – and go on up the good track, passing below glorious beeches and ancient yews. After half a mile follow the signpost directing you left along a concessionary path to Warton Crag. Stroll the

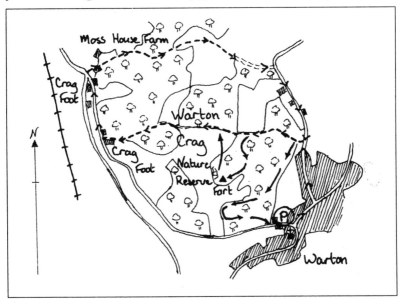

The view from Warton Crag

delightful path for half a mile to reach the trig. point and then an elevated metal brazier.

This is the site of the original beacon that announced the sighting of the Spanish Armada in 1588. Here too warning was received by beacon from Birkrigg, in Furness, of the approach of the marauding Scots. Sit on the huge limestone boulders and enjoy the grand view over Morecambe Bay – south to the Fylde, east to Ingleborough and north to the Lakeland fells. This extensive view over the sands would have been familiar to our iron age ancestors whose 7-acre hillfort, enclosed by 15 acres of outer ramparts, occupied this lofty site. Below you can see across the Keer Channel to Carnforth, with its railway sheds and sidings. About the top grow many blackthorn bushes, a

Chimney of old Pumping Station

cloud of white in early spring and, in September, laden with purple sloes.

Retrace your steps to a signpost just after the trig. point and take the left branch, signed Crag Foot. The narrow path, over limestone boulders, comes to a huge kissing gate, where you turn left. The way now continues through a bracken-clad clearing in birch woodland. Go on to pass through the next gate to rejoin the original bridleway. Turn left and descend the glorious track. Look and listen for goldcrests and coal tits in the fir plantation on your right. They are present whatever time of year you walk this way.

Saunter on until you reach the road at Crag Foot, where you turn right. Walk the quiet road to the telephone box. Beyond take the rough wide track going off right. Pass a tall restored chimney, part of the old pumping engine which drained the mosses so that they could be used for agriculture.

Just before the farm take the signposted track on the right. Thirty yards on, turn left to pass through a waymarked gap into woodland. Go through the gate to emerge into pasture and follow the track to a gate on your right.

Beyond, climb through more woodland to take the left of two gates. Continue on the clear track to climb a waymarked stile. Go on ahead along the grassy way, with a wall to the left. Pass to the left of a huge oak with a footpath sign nailed to it. Proceed in the same general direction to climb through trees to a squeeze stile in a wall. Beyond, walk ahead to join a track, where you turn left. Stay with the gated track until you reach the Coach Road once more.

Turn right and steadily descend. Turn into the bridleway on your right, taken earlier. A few yards along, go through the squeeze stile into the nature reserve, 200 acres of limestone crags, grassland and woodland. Follow the narrow path, rough in parts, from where you might see a red squirrel. The glorious way goes on and on, generally keeping close to a wall on your left. Pass through a tight squeeze stile in the wall ahead. Stay with the wall to your left for a short distance and then, where the path swings right, go down a rough slope. Turn left and pass through another squeeze stile. Descend the continuing path through woodland, with the sheer limestone cliffs of the old quarry to your left, to rejoin your car.

Goldcrest

9. Jenny Brown's Point

Yealand Storrs – Summer House Hill – Crag Foot – Jenny Brown's Point – Jack Scout – Silverdale Green – Gait Barrows reserve – Yealand Storrs.

Start/Finish: Wide verge close to the junction of roads at the north-west end of Yealand Storrs (GR 494761). Yealand Storrs lies 11½ miles south of Kendal, west of the A6.

Type of Walk: A varied 8½-mile circular walk through the glorious parkland of Leighton Hall and on to the lovely limestone shore at Jenny Brown's Point and Jack Scout. It returns through woods with limestone scars and pavement almost hidden by crag-fast yews and hazel copses.

Map: OS Pathfinder 636 SD 37/47 Grange-over-Sands

The Walk

Yealand Storrs, where this walk starts, lies close to flat pastures and mosses. Here grew acres of flax used, with hemp, by the villagers of the Yealands for spinning yarn needed to weave coarse cloth and ticking for mattress and pillow covers.

From the wide verge walk south to cross the road signposted Silverdale. Walk on for 150 yards, toward Yealand Storrs, to take the first signposted footpath on the right. Follow the farm track as it swings right through pastures. Here you are likely to see a buzzard, green woodpecker and jay. Away to the right you can see Leighton Moss RSPB reserve, its blue pools surrounded in August by a haze of rose-bay willow-herb. At the end of the track, join the access road to Leighton Hall, where you turn left. Continue past the white-walled mansion with its turrets and battlements.

The hall is owned by Major and Mrs Reynolds, descendants of the Gillows of furniture fame. Its story started in 1246 as a fortified manor on land granted to Adam D'Avranches by

William de Lancaster, Baron of Kendal, in 1173. In 1763 a George Townley had the house rebuilt in Adam style, the park laid out and the woods replanted.

Take the signposted footpath that climbs left up the slope to the seat on Summer House Hill, the latter topped with a row of stately beeches. Pause here to enjoy the magnificent view over the hall, the mosses and the bay. Follow the good track, right (south), through the trees to the road, where you turn right. Walk the quiet road and, just beyond the sharp left turn, stride the cart track (unsignposted) on your right.

Walk for nearly half a mile through woodland. Don't miss the footpath leading off right to an easy-to-miss squeeze stile in a wall. The stile is just before a large white sign on a tree, on the continuing track. Drop down through trees to pass to the right

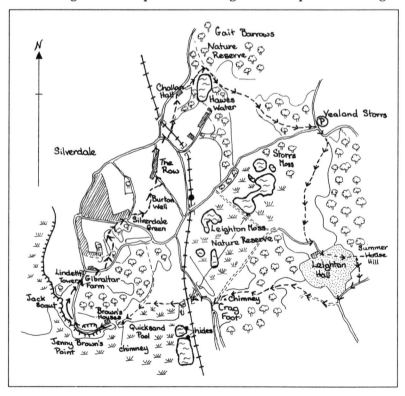

of a huge oak which supports a footpath sign. Head on towards a gate. Do not pass through but follow the track, which swings left.

Go on over waymarked stiles, with woodland to your right. Follow the track through more woodland, and then where the way swings left to a stile. Beyond, walk through trees to take a signposted path on the right. Continue to a track and turn right. (This mile-long stretch of the walk was completed, in the opposite direction, in walk 8).

At the road turn left to pass the tall chimney of the old steam pump. Until 1917 it was linked with dykes that drained the mosses so that it could be used for agriculture.

Join the main road and turn right. After 300 yard, turn left just before Quicksand Pool Bridge. Pass under the railway bridge. Go on a few yards. Here you might like to leave the walk and turn left to stroll to the Alan and Eric Morecambe bird hide. Take your binoculars and watch for whimbrel, greenshank, curlew sandpipers and godwits.

Greenshank and Black-tailed Godwits

Return to the path, turn right and cross the dyke to pass through a gate. Stroll left across the stiled pastures to a four-armed signpost at the foot of wooded slopes. These drop down to a shore strewn with limestone boulders.

Across the Kent Estuary from Jack Scout

Continue west along the lovely coastline, following the sign-post for Jenny Brown's point. Away to your left stretches saltmarsh bisected by tidal gutters. Pass another tall chimney, this one part of an old limekiln, and then on below Brown's houses. It is believed that Jenny Brown lived here about 250 years ago. Little is known about her, other than she kept pigs.

Join a narrow hedged lane which leads to the point. Sit on the seat, enjoy the glorious panorama and ponder on the 18th century Jenny who gave her name to this delightful corner. In 1864 a line of boulders, extending from the point out into the sands for about a mile, was part of a scheme put forward to reclaim Silverdale Sands. The cost was to have been £84,000. Parliament approved of the scheme but the House of Lords did not and the plan was abandoned. The line of boulders was left to the sea birds.

Walk on along the hedged lane which is festooned by travel-

Old lime kiln, Jack Scout

ler's joy, a lime-loving climbing plant. Listen as you go for the calls of curlews and oyster catchers. Pass through a kissing gate on the left to walk Jack Scout. This is a pleasing area of limestone vegetation, stretching away to the oak clad low cliffs overlooking the great expanse of Morecambe Bay. Jack Scout was acquired in 1982 by the National Trust. Here wander at will. All paths lead back to a gate to the road, beside which stands a huge restored limekiln

Go on along the lane to pass Lindeth Tower, a folly, where Elizabeth Gaskell, author and biographer of Charlotte Brontë, and her daughters often stayed. From the sitting room at the top, they watched travellers crossing the sands.

At the T-junction, just beyond Gibraltar farm, turn right. After 300 yards take the signposted left turn into woodland. Stride the upper path, along a limestone terrace, into more extensive woodland. Then go on to a grassy area where you bear left to a stile. Beyond, follow the clear way through trees from where, all year round, nuthatches call. The path and then the track lead to the road at Silverdale Green.

Turn right and walk on to take Bottoms Lane, on the left, in the direction of Arnside. Look for the track on the right, signposted Burton Well, along which you stride. Pass several houses and then move into woodland and follow the wall round left to come to the walled well. Walk on into a pasture almost surrounded by woodland. Dawdle on and then turn right to cross a wooden footbridge and continue over Lambert's Meadow, to a ladderstile into trees.

The way continues left, up two flights of limestone steps, to the road. Turn left and walk 600 yards along the quiet lane. Then turn right and, at the T-junction, walk ahead in the direction of Carnforth and take the footpath on the left, signposted Challon Hall. Walk ahead to cross the railway line and go on along the English Nature signposted footpath. Aim for the hall and take a stile on its left. Walk ahead to the road.

Turn right and take the next footpath on the right, for Yealand Storrs. Here a board welcomes you to Gait Barrows. Stride the pleasant path through the lovely national nature reserve, 170 acres of limestone pavement, typically eroded into clints and grykes, where grow yew, ash, hazel, wych elm, privet, hawthorn, rowan and holly.

Bear right at the footpath sign. Walk close to Hawes Water, which is fringed with rushes, where once 9-inch char were caught. Legend tells that the lake once was the haunt of a fearsome serpent.

Climb the stile at the path end and bear diagonally right across a large pasture. Cross a derelict wall and continue to a very high ladderstile. Beyond, maintain the same general direction to a grey metal gate (ignore the red one) into woodland. Go on to join, and walk right, a gated track from where you can see Storrs Moss and Leighton Hall. At the road, turn left to rejoin your car.

10. Arnside

Arnside – Blackstone Point – Arnside Tower – Arnside Knott – Arnside

Start/Finish: Parking area at the far end of the promenade (south-west) at Arnside. There are many parking spaces but they are quickly occupied, so get there early (GR 452785). Leave Kendal by the A6 and drive south to Milnthorpe. Turn right at the traffic lights in the centre of the village and continue through Sandside and Storth to Arnside. (9 miles south of Kendal).

Type of Walk: An enjoyable circular walk of 6½ miles with something to please all the family; a saunter along the glorious sands of the Kent Estuary, a stroll through delightful woodland on the edge of cliffs, generally colourful with a host of limestone-loving plants, and a steady climb to the top of Arnside Knott with a spectacular view to complete the day.

Map: OS Pathfinder 636 SD 37/47 Grange-over-Sands

The Kent Estuary with viaduct, Arnside

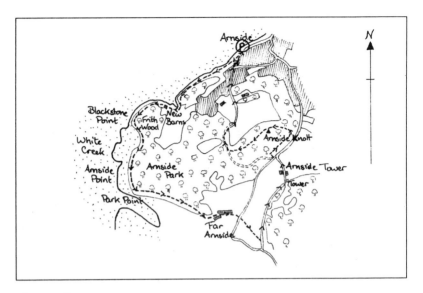

The Walk

Arnside overlooks the calm waters of Morecambe Bay. Consult tide tables in the local newspaper and chose a time when the tide is out for most of the day if you wish to walk along the delightful sands.

From the parking area take the signposted footpath to New Barns, which continues ahead (south-west)from the end of the promenade. Out on the sands, watch for long-billed oyster catchers and a variety of gulls probing the mud. Regularly shelduck sieve through the water of tidal gutters. To your left steep wooded slopes tower upwards. Look across the colourful estuary to see the town of Grange strung out along the opposite bank.

At New Barns, follow the indistinct path as it moves inland for a few hundred yards and then swings back out towards the shore again. In spring enjoy the great variety of wild flowers along the way, including cowslips, red campion, marsh orchid and wild strawberry.

Here you have a choice of taking the good track that cuts off Blackstone Point, passing along the south side of Frith Wood,

or of going round the shoreline that edges Frith Wood. Both are very pleasant. The two ways unite at the far end of White Creek. If on the shore look for an easy way (well used) up the shallow cliffs to join the path that continues through woodland along the cliffs. Stroll on among the trees around Arnside Point and Park Point. In late spring look

Lily-of-the Valley and Rock Rose

here for extensive areas of lily-of-the-valley and rock rose. At the signpost continue on in the direction of Far Arnside.

More than a century ago passengers who wished to journey across the sands in the stagecoach from Hest Bank to Kents Bank walked out from this little village to board it.

At the end of the woodland, take the left-hand branch, where the continuing road divides. This passes through a caravan site and then goes along a narrow road. At the T-junction, cross with care and follow the footpath signposted Silverdale. Pass through two gates as you traverse the delightful pastures and then follow a waymark up through trees to a narrow road. Turn left and, after 400 yards, take the continuing pebbled track to the left of the road.

Suddenly the gaunt ruins of Arnside Tower appear ahead, almost 50 feet high. What a magnificent site was chosen, one guarding the valley that runs inland from the sea. The tower, constructed of limestone, is believed to have been built in the 14th century by the de Broughton family against invasion from sea or land. It was destroyed by storm and fire in 1602.

Arnside Tower

Pass through a gate and follow the track that swings left to pass to the left of Arnside Tower farm, where swallows nest in summer. Stride the access lane to the road, which you cross. Go through the gate into the National Trust's Arnside Knott Wood. Walk the wide track to take the first path that climbs through the trees on your right. On joining a track go on in the same direction, taking a left branch each time there is a choice, until you come to a wall. Climb steadily up beside it, through the pleasing woodland, until you near a three-armed signpost. Ignore this and bear left, gradually climbing. At the ridge, follow the track left to walk along the top of the Knott (159m).

The high hill is composed of limestone, a hard resistant rock formed from the skeletons of innumerable corals and sea lilies, which lived in warm seas 300 million years ago. Stride the airy top to a seat with magnificent views over to the Lakeland hills and the estuary.

Continue on to see an unusual H-shaped tree. Legend has it that in 1882 a seaman and his young bride twisted the narrow stems of young saplings together in a lover's knot. The trees flourished to form two curious arches like a letter H.

Go on until the track divides, where you take the right branch to come to three view indicators, which detail the magnificence all around. Drop down the slope on a narrow path to join a reinforced track, where you turn right. The way soon becomes metalled and continues descending towards Arnside, passing a large convalescent home on your left.

Stride on and, at the T-junction, bear right. Take the second footpath on the left, signposted Promenade. Once on the Promenade, turn right to rejoin your car.

11. Levens Park

Levens Park – River Kent – Levens Park

Start/Finish: Park in large layby on the west side of the A6, north of Levens Bridge (GR 488854). To reach this layby, leave Kendal by the by-pass (A591) and drive south to the Sedgwick round-about to join the A590 (Barrow exit). After a quarter of a mile follow the A6 slip road, on the left. Levens Park lies four miles from Kendal.

Type of Walk: This is a delectable, easy, 3-mile walk, which takes you through the famous deer park and beside the petulant River Kent. You might like to combine the walk with a visit to the lovely old house and garden with its famous topiary. You are asked to avoid disturbing the animals, to stay on the paths and keep dogs on leads.

Map: OS Pathfinder 627 SD 48/59 Milnthorpe. There is a map of the park at the entrance.

Bagot goats, Levens Park

The Walk

In 1790 Thomas West in his "Guide to the Lakes" described Levens Park as "the sweetest spot that Fancy can imagine". The park, part of a medieval deer park, lies on the other side of the A6 from Levens Hall. It was landscaped by Gillaume Beaumont, who also designed the garden of the Hall.

In the park graze deer and goats. The deer are rare Norwegian black fallow. They are in fact very dark brown in colour. Sometimes a white fawn is born, and when this happens, local superstition says that some change will take place in the Hall.

The Bagot goats are also a rare breed which the owners of Levens Hall are trying to maintain and encourage.

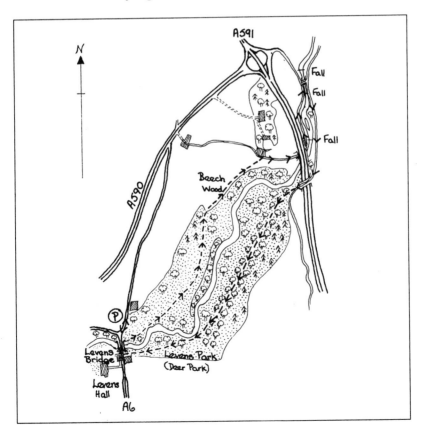

Gateway to Levens Hall

A ghost said to haunt the Hall is supposed to be that of a gypsy woman who was refused food and died of starvation. Before she did so, she prophesied that no son should inherit the Hall until the river ceased to flow and a white fawn was born. Oddly, Levens Hall passed continuously through the female line until 1896. Then Alan Bagot was born, the river froze over and a white fawn was born to the herd in the park.

Take the signposted footpath, on the left (west), before the bridge, to walk through the lovely park. Stride the waymarked

The River Kent at Levens Bridge

footpath to its end and then climb the stone steps over a wall. Turn right and continue on the stiled way, along the edge of Beech Wood, to join a metalled road. Turn right to come beside dramatic river scenery.

Here the River Kent descends in magnificent falls. This is the site of an 18th century iron forge. Here the sound of large hammers beating pig iron would have drowned the sound of the roaring water.

Pass below the Kendal by-pass on a raised walkway, high above the surging water. Continue on to cross a bridge over the exuberant river and turn right at the T-junction. Follow the road as it bears right to cross back above the by-pass. A few yards on, on the right, pass through a gate back into the park. Bear left to dawdle the continuing footpath, now south of the Kent.

The path, well waymarked, passes below the oaks of the

famous avenue planted by Beaumont. Wherever trees died, replacements were planted within their rotten stumps to maintain the integrity of Beaumont's design.

The mile-long avenue, once the original carriage drive, continues towards the Hall. About the park trees, have been planted in natural groupings. Elsewhere woodlands have been allowed to follow the curves of the river valley. Look for the deer and goats. They roam the park in a landscape little changed over the centuries.

Towards the end of the avenue a sign directs you right and then ahead, the continuing footpath returning you to the A6. Turn right to rejoin your car.

12. Whitbarrow

Mill Side – Lord's Seat – Rawson's Wood – Raven's Lodge –
Mill Side

Start/Finish: Layby for parking, just beyond the old road, north
side of the A590, signposted Mill Side and Beck Head (GR
453839). To reach this spot, leave Kendal by the by-pass,
travelling south, and take the A590 for Barrow.

Type of Walk: This glorious 7½-mile circular walk takes you first
to Lord's Seat, at 706 feet the highest point on Whitbarrow. The
top of its scar is an airy, extensive stretch of limestone pavement,
with many smaller scarps, clints and grykes. On it grow vast
clumps of juniper, crag-fast yews, heather, silver birch and ash.
The magnificent scar rivets the attention of travellers on the A590
and, for those on their way home to South Cumbria, it provides
a wonderful and familiar welcome. The walk then continues
through mixed woodland, returning along delightful tracks below
flaring limestone walls. Good walking underfoot. All ascents climb
steadily.

Map: OS Pathfinder 627 SD 48/59 Milnthorpe

The Walk

From the layby walk on into Mill Side. Keep to the right fork,
where the road branches, and turn right again immediately, just
beyond the telephone box. Climb steadily past the farm, with
its barn on your left. It is a bank barn, a kind rarely found
outside Cumbria and the Yorkshire Dales. Such barns have a
ramp, natural or artificial, on one side which gives access to an
upper storey where hay is stored. On the other side there is
access to a lower storey, where the cattle are held. A trapdoor
between the two storeys allows fodder to be fed easily to the
animals below.

Ignore the footpath going off on the left and continue a short

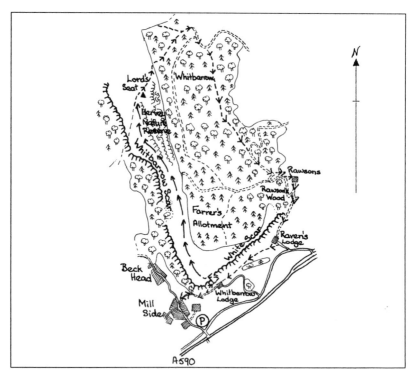

distance to take the permissive path (arrowed in white), on the left, which climbs steadily into glorious woodland. The sides of the path are reinforced with large stones heavily encrusted with moss. At a junction of paths continue in the same general direction (right) until you reach a clearing in the trees, a seat and another waymark. Pause here to enjoy the view of the dramatic meanders of the River Kent as it heads for its estuary.

Bear left, up through the trees, as directed by the arrow. After a steady climb (west) follow the waymark that directs you left, to walk by a wall on your right, and then another arrow pointing to a gap in the wall. A clear path continues through birch woodland and then moves up onto the open fell. As you gently ascend, look right to see the Howgills. Follow the cairned way as you bear north, coming closer to a conifer plantation. Here look left for a spectacular view of Morecambe Bay and the Leven

Canon Hervey Memorial Cairn

Viaduct. Suddenly, ahead, the Lakeland mountains come into view. Look down over the scar edge to see the stately, castellated Witherslack Hall deep in its woodland.

Follow the clear path as it comes close to the trees of the plantation and then climb the ladder stile into the Flodder Allotment. A large wall encloses the Hervey Nature Reserve. In 1962 Canon G. A. K. Hervey was largely responsible for the foundation of the Lake District Naturalists' Trust.

Walk the lovely way, past clints and grykes and many shallow scars to ascend to Lord's Seat. Here a tablet, built into a splendid cairn, commemorates Canon Hervey's efforts. In 1969 two years after his death, the area became a nature reserve. In 1995 Cumbria Wildlife Trust repaired the boundary walls and provided information signs. With the introduction of sheep grazing the encroachment of scrub has been restricted.

After enjoying the view, go on to descend the slope. Walk on to take a sturdy stepped stile in the splendid limestone wall on your right, which edges woodland. Stride ahead on a good path through larch, yew, hazel, birch and Scots pine. At a T-junction of paths, bear left and follow the wide path through the quiet woodland. At a junction of paths, where several huge old oaks grow, turn right and then, at a meeting of several paths, turn right again to climb steadily for 50 yards, following the waymark. At yet another junction of paths, walk ahead, taking the lower waymarked path past a huge yew on the left.

Carry on along the track, to join a reinforced forest track where you follow the waymark, right. Look out for the place where the track passes through a gateless wall and, just beyond, turn left as directed by an easy-to-miss arrow. This track drops steadily downhill, rapidly coming beside a wall with pasture beyond. As you descend you can look across the flat pastures of the Lyth Valley, through which flows the River Gilpin.

Nuthatch

The Lyth Valley is well known for its damson trees. One theory is that these originated from Damascus. Another is that the monks of Cartmel developed them by grafting the wild sloe onto the plum, the result being sometimes called the bullace. The berries provided dye for the woollen trade. In late spring the valley is white with blossom.

Follow the path as it turns acutely right. Look here for nuthatches in the trees. Continue where the path swings left and then continues ahead to pass to the left of Rawson's farm. Turn right before the last building to walk a fenced track below Rawson's Wood and then White Scar.

Go on along the delightful way, with trees to the right and a pretty stream to the left, where hart's tongue fern thrives. The fronds of this fern are undivided and strap-shaped, quite unlike what one expects of a fern. It is a plant of shady limestone walls and limestone pavement, in the deep fissures of which windblown soil settles. In the sheltered and humid conditions of these hollows, where sheep cannot graze, the fern flourishes.

Continue on the now metalled road as it bears left to pass Raven's Lodge and then take the signposted bridleway on the right. This climbs steadily uphill under great beech trees, with the gleaming white face of the scar towering upwards.

Stroll on where the track becomes a path. Carry on past the dwellings, on your left, called Whitbarrow Lodge on the map. Then you pass the permissive path taken at the start of the walk. Continue downhill into Mill Side, turn left and walk down the lane to rejoin your car.

Whitbarrow from Mill Side

13. Latterbarrow

Latterbarrow nature reserve – High Fell End – Witherslack Hall farm – nature reserve

Start/Finish: Park along the edge of the old road (GR 432827) close to the nature reserve. To reach this area leave Kendal by the by-pass and join the A590 at the Sedgwick roundabout. After 5½-miles take the right turn, signposted Witherslack, and quickly turn left beyond the Derby Arms. The start of the walk lies 7 miles from Kendal.

Type of Walk: This 6-mile circular walk starts at the small nature reserve, a glorious flower-bedecked haven of peace, just off the noisy A590. It continues through delectable deciduous woodland for much of the way, with occasional glimpses, through trees, of the pleasing Winster Valley and the long pale hump of Whitbarrow Scar. It is easy walking for much of the way, with a steady climb to Yewbarrow. Parts of the route are signposted. After rain the paths through woodland can be muddy. Strong shoes essential

Map: OS Pathfinder 627 SD 48/59 Milnthorpe

The Walk

From the side of the old road, take the footpath on the west side, signposted High Fell End. Pass through the gate into Latterbarrow nature reserve. Follow the waymark, right. If you visit in May you will see a vast array of cowslips, violets, primroses, marsh orchids, salad burnet and bird's foot trefoil. From the trees, at this time, come the urgent calls of blackcap, willow warbler, blackbird, long tailed tit and chaffinch.

Follow the waymarks to pass beside hawthorns, heavy with blossom in the spring and laden with berries in the autumn, and go through a gate into pasture. To the right stands Whitbarrow Scar the high ridge that shelters this lovely part of Cumbria from damaging winds. Continue beside a wall on the left. Take

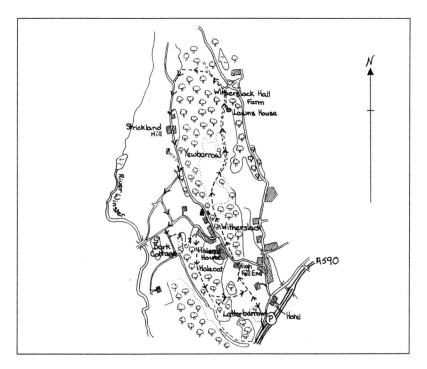

the waymarked gate ahead, which lies to the right of a tied gate, to pass between the cottages of High Fell End.

At Church Road, turn left and walk uphill to take the public bridleway to Witherslack Hall. Ascend steadily through the delightful woodland, for nearly half a mile. Look for woodruff growing below the trees. To the right the wooded limestone slopes rear upwards and to the left descend steeply.

Ignore the waymarked left turn that drops downhill. Two hundred yards on, take one of the several tracks leading left, uphill, to an open area. From here enjoy the extensive view over the Winster Valley, equally famous as the Lyth Valley (walk 12) for its damson trees.

Perhaps this is the place for a coffee stop.

Return to the path through the trees and saunter on, ignoring side turns, to come to a gate and a stile to the pastures on Yewbarrow (128m). Bear slightly right as you continue along a

Whitbarrow from Yewbarrow

wide grassy track, with limestone outcrops to the left. Look right for glimpses of the Kent Estuary.

Proceed along a reinforced track, with pastures to the right and woodland to the left. Go on across a wide pasture encircled by trees to pass in front of Lawns House. Enter more woodland, walking on a walled, well reinforced track. At the T-junction, to the right you can see the outbuildings of Witherslack Hall farm. Dean Barwick lived at Witherslack Hall and died in 1664. In his will he left money for the repair of the old chapel at St Mary's, near the hall, and for a new burial ground. Until then the dead had to be carried across the dangerous Milnthorpe Sands to be interred at the mother church of Beetham.

Turn left to stride on through more woodland, again ignoring all side turns. Where the wood ends, a walled track descends, bearing left, beside coppiced hazel to join a quiet lane. Turn left and walk the delightful hedged way to pass through the hamlet of Strickland Hill. Go on and, where the lane divides, take the right branch. Continue to a track, leading off left, to walk the very straight grassy way.

Gate, St Paul's Church, Witherslack

At the road, turn right and continue a short distance to take a 'no through road' on the left. Just before Bark Cottage, take the track, signposted Halecat, on the left. Climb the stile to the left of the cottage, follow the wall round right to an easy-to-miss stone stepped stile on the right. Go ahead, bearing slightly left, to follow an indistinct track that climbs steadily through trees. At the top of the slope, go on with the wall to your right. Follow the track as it moves from the wall into woodland.

Continue beside the fence on the left until you reach a boundary fence. Here you may like to make a diversion left to visit the well proportioned church of St. Paul, Witherslack. It

Cowslips

was consecrated in 1671. Look for the finely carved pulpit and the sun dial in the churchyard.

To continue the walk, return to the boundary fence and go on right (south) to climb a stile and begin a lovely stroll along a clear way, through more woodland. Continue ahead, imperceptibly descending for nearly a mile, until you reach a three-armed signpost. Take the left turn, to climb a stile on the left. Walk ahead through the trees, which in spring are perfumed with sweet briar, to a stone stile. Beyond join an indistinct grassy way, bear left and then, almost immediately, right, to a waymarked gate which is difficult to spot.

Walk along beside the fence and climb the waymarked stile on the right. Walk on, in the same general direction, to pass through a waymarked gateless gap and continue beside the walled woodland on the left. Pass through a gate and take another, almost opposite, and stride on to cross a splendid footbridge. Pause here to look left to see Halecat House. Stroll on along the track and follow it as it swings right to join the bridleway taken at the start of the walk. Stride on to rejoin your car.

14. Bowland Bridge

Bowland Bridge – Hubbersty Head – Bryan House farm –
Birks Bridge – Great Hartbarrow – Bowland Bridge

Start/Finish: Large layby north of the telephone box, the post office and the petrol pumps at the hamlet of Bowland Bridge (GR 418897). The hamlet is 5 miles from Kendal and is reached by quiet lanes through an upland area of great beauty.

Type of Walk: The Winster Valley runs parallel with Windermere, lying to its south-east side and separated from it by Gummers How and Cartmell Fell. It has some of England's most delightful countryside – rolling pastures, quiet paths and tracks, deciduous woodland full of birds, dancing becks, trim hedgerows, pleasing bridges and attractive rocky outcrops. This 6-mile circular walk takes you through the valley with barely a car or another person to be met.

Maps: OS Pathfinder 627 SD 48/58 Milnthorpe. OS Outdoor Leisure 7 The English Lakes, South Eastern area.

The Walk

From the parking area, walk back past the post office and take the left turn, signposted Witherslack and Grange. After a hundred yards, climb the signposted stepped stile on the left. Stride ahead to the interesting stile in the corner ahead, which spans a junction of four walls. Beyond the next ladderstile, ahead, go on in line with the telegraph poles, keeping to the left of a barn, to a stile to a road.

Cross and turn left to take the signposted gate now on your right. Walk on to cross Arndale Beck and go on to pass through a stile beside a gate. Turn left when you have climbed almost to the next gate, to walk to a stile in the wall, two-thirds of the way along. Beyond drop slightly left to a gap in the far left corner. Stride right very quickly to come beside a wall on your

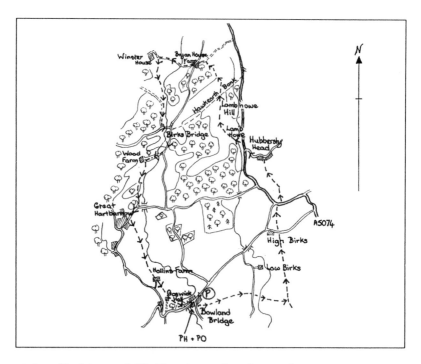

right, climbing uphill. Continue ahead over three more pastures to the road. To the right you can see the church at Crosthwaite.

Crosthwaite is a hilly village, sometimes known as Church Town. Crosthwaite means a cross in a clearing and there was a church here long before St Mary's was built in 1878-9. The church has no side aisles.

Take the signposted stile on the opposite side of the road and climb gently beside the wall on your left. Look right to glimpse the mushroom-shaped shelter on Scout Scar. Closer on the right is Tarnside and its large blue pool. Stroll ahead from the stile to the road.

Turn right and take the signposted footpath on the left. Pass several of Winster's famed damson trees and climb the slope to join a cart track which swings right in front of a cottage. Before a small stone barn, turn left and walk with a wall to your right. Pass through a gate. Beyond, continue ahead to another gate

Scots Pine, Hawkearth Bank

and then continue beside a hedge on your left to take a stile in the far left corner. Continue on with the hedge now to your right. Cross two stiles and then over an access track to a stile to the road. Dawdle left, with Hubbersty Head to your right.

At the T-junction, turn right and then take the track on the left, signposted Lamb Howe and Hawkearth Bank. Pass Lamb Howe on your left and go on to the waymarked gate ahead. Here you might see bullfinches in the hedgerow.

Stride on to the rather high ladderstile to join a grassy track, with a young plantation full of whispering goldcrests, to the left, and a hedge to the right. Look for the pleasing lake, fringed with trees, to your left. Climb the stile on your right and continue on in the same direction to a stile that requires a large stride to surmount it.

Beyond continue up the slope, veering slightly right. Pause to enjoy the splendid views. To keep to the right of way, ignore the continuing wide grassy swathe and walk a narrower lower grassy path, which runs parallel to it, to a waymarked post. From here swing left to the side of walled woodland to join the grassy swathe seen earlier. Turn right and carry on with the wood to your left. Walk on the track beside a second walled woodland. Look right to see Winster church. Holy Trinity, a grey church of Westmorland slate, was built in 1875 a little apart from the scattered village. It replaced an earlier one built close by.

Join the road and turn left. The farm here is known as Bryan House. From 1682 to 1720 it was the home of Jonas Barber, a famous clockmaker. Walk for 100 yards to a signposted right turn, to stroll along a private drive. Pass the vicarage and cross the River Winster. The river used to form the county boundary between Lancashire and Westmorland. It rises on Brantfell and empties its water into the estuary at Grange.

Walk ahead towards Winster House and then, just before it, turn left to walk a wide grassy track that swings away left. At the corner of woodland continue ahead, veering slightly left to a stile in the wall. Continue on. Look right to see a huge limekiln. Limestone was burnt in kilns to produce lime, used extensively by farmers to improve their sour acidic soils.

Carry on to join a farm track, where you walk left. Ignore the footbridge on the left and stride on to the road. Turn left and continue to cross the delightful Birks Bridge, a clapper bridge constructed of huge slabs of slate. Beside the bridge is a deepish ford.

Turn right. Walk the quiet lane and turn right onto a bridle-way signposted Wood farm and Hartbarrow Lane. Keep to the left of the farm and leave the walled track by a gate on the left. Pass through the gate ahead, step across a small beck and walk on to the lower edge of a copse on the right. Stroll a short walled track and stride ahead to the side of another copse to continue along a cart track to the road. Turn right and, just before the cottages at Great Hartbarrow, take the bridleway to Hollins farm on the left.

Pass through the gate ahead to walk with the wall to your right. Pass through the next gate, halfway along the boundary wall ahead. Carry on into a walled track and step across a shallow ford, where you might see a grey wagtail perched on one of the stepping stones. Carry on to the Hollins House, which you pass to the left.

Turn left through a wicket gate to go below a large telegraph pole to take another gate. Turn right and pass through the next stile. Head left across the pasture to a stile between two young sycamores. Walk on, with Goswick Hall to the right and a magnificent view of Whitbarrow Scar ahead. Bear right through a small wood. The indistinct path is waymarked on trees, but if wet underfoot, find the driest way. Emerge at the far right corner, with Bowland Bridge ahead. A kissing gate beside the lovely bridge gives access to the hamlet. Stand on the bridge and read that you are now on the boundary between Westmorland (Crosthwaite and Lyth) and Lancashire (Cartmell Fell). Walk left to rejoin your car.

Birks Bridge

15. Scout Scar and Cunswick Scar

Kendal – Scout Scar – Cunswick Scar – Kendal

Start/Finish: This 7-mile circular walk starts from the Town Hall, Kendal

Type of Walk: In just under a mile you can be striding over fine limestone hill country, from where there are magnificent views. It is all easy walking, but limestone and woodland paths can be slippery after rain, so use sensible footwear.

Map: OS outdoor Leisure 7, The English Lakes, South Eastern area

---

The Walk

Leave the town by Allhallows Lane, which climbs steeply uphill opposite the Town Hall. At the crossroads at the top, turn

left and then right to continue along Brigsteer Road. Cross Kendal by-pass and take the second footpath on the right, signposted Scout Scar and Barrowfield. Look for the old cast-iron signpost, dated 1900, standing by the stile.

Stroll the grassy path, bearing half-left across Kendal's old racecourse. Pass through an iron kissing gate onto the limestone fell, which is scattered with juniper and holly. Follow the good track, steadily climbing, to pass through a stone stepped stile. From here you can see the flat top of Ingleborough in Yorkshire.

Juniper

Gap stile and milestone on Brigsteer Road

The way continues through heather, yew and scrubby thorn bushes and from the brow of the scar you have a dramatic view of the Lakeland hills. Continue past a large cairn and approach the scar edge, slightly downhill, with care. Below lies the lovely Lyth Valley, with its white houses and small hamlets set amid the rolling pastures.

Turn right and go along the magnificent escarpment with its closely cropped turf. Just beyond the highest point is Hodgson's Leap, where cragfast hollies and ash grow in steep gullies running almost perpendicularly to the clearing and woodland far below.

Bear right along a narrow path to visit the mushroom-shaped shelter, which is also a view indicator. From here you have a panoramic view, including Black Combe, the Coniston Fells, the Langdales, the Scafells, the High Street mountains, the Shap Fells, the Howgills, the Yorkshire hills and the Kent Estuary.

Return to the scar edge and continue onwards. Just before you descend to the fell road, pause to see Cunswick Tarn and Cunswick Hall. The latter lies in the parish of Underbarrow. It was once a pele tower and is now a farmhouse. An ancient packhorse route from Kendal came over Cunswick Scar and past this very old house.

Beyond the kissing gate, turn right and walk uphill, with care, to pass the car park in an old quarry. Go on to take a signposted permissive track on the left, leading towards a tall police mast in a copse of trees.

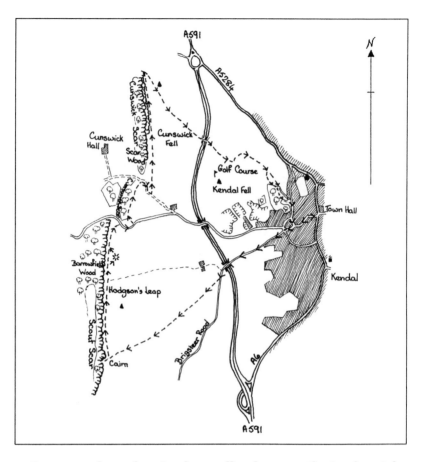

Carry on through mixed woodland to a stile in the right corner. Continue with the wall to the left and, at the boundary corner, turn right, still with the wall to your left. Notice the very pale grey limestone walls, each stone showing parallel lines of erosion.

Pass the four-armed signpost, continue to the corner of the wall and take the public footpath for Cunswick Scar. Stride on, following the path, over a stile and then steadily climb the walled Scar. To your left, Scar Wood drops steeply down. Look through the trees to see again the tarn and the hall.

Head on along the unfenced side of the scar, where juniper

Scout Scar

grows above tall yew trees, with ash, holly and birch below, until you reach a stile. Do not cross. Turn acutely right to climb to the cairn on Cunswick Fell. Head on along the broad top of the fell and then descend a green trod to a waymarked stile in a wall. The stile stands to the left of a hawthorn tree and at the angle of two walls. Continue across the pasture to a stiled footbridge over the by-pass. Beyond, walk straight uphill, pass-

ing through a stile to a signpost on the golf course on Kendal
Fell. A series of signposts takes you safely across. Follow the
waymark, directing you left, downhill, beside the wall and then
continue where it swings right, through trees. Pass through an
old quarry and dawdle along the good track.

Below to your left lie the greystone houses of Kendal. At a
junction of paths, take the right branch, continuing towards
some well placed seats from where you can enjoy the grand
view. Then stroll on into the Serpentine Woods, where several
small paths lead down towards Kendal. At the road, continue
downhill to return to the Town Hall.

16. Winster

Winster – Winster House – Rosthwaite Heights – Barker Knott farm – Bow Mabble Breast – Winster

Start/Finish: Park in a large layby north-west of the Brown Horse public house, Winster (GR 418936). To reach this scattered village, which lies 5 miles from Kendal, leave the town by the Underbarrow Road, continue through Crosthwaite and turn right onto the A5074 for Winster.

Type of Walk: This is a grand 7½-mile circular walk with many fine views. It takes you through peaceful pastures, along quiet lanes and close to charming farmhouses, where time seems to have stood still.

Map: OS Outdoor Leisure 7, The English Lakes, South Eastern area

---

The Walk

Winster lies in such a quiet corner of Cumbria that it is easy to pass by without noticing. It is composed of scattered stone cottages, some white-washed, many with a slate-hung porch and most with a small orchard of damson trees. The village has an inn and a church and once had a school. Winster takes it name from the river that rises on Brant Fell, flows through the village and into its estuary at Grange-over-Sands.

From the layby, cross the A-road and take the hedged and fenced lane leading off it, signposted Birkett Houses. Stride out into pleasing pastures where you might spot a heron feeding in one of the small streams. As the lane begins to climb, and just before a wood, straddle the stile on the left and edge the woodland to pass through a gate. Beyond strike diagonally left across a large pasture to join a track. Go through the gate and bear left to a kissing gate to join another walled track.

To the left, almost hidden by conifers, stands Birkett Houses.

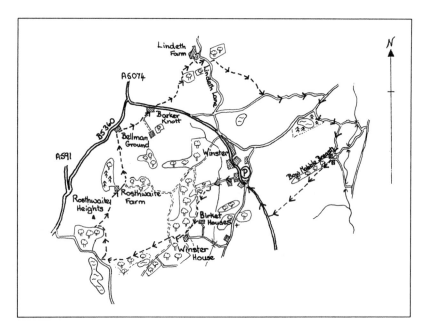

Its front lawn has dramatic topiary. Continue on to Winster House and turn right before the dwelling to walk the delightful walled and gated track. Here you might hear and see goldcrests in the trees on the slopes.

Pass through a gate onto the open fell, with good views of the Coniston range ahead, often snow-topped in winter. Bear left for two or three paces and then take the waymarked grassy track, bearing due west. Stride along the lovely fell track, beside which scattered Swaledales patiently graze the rough grass. These sheep, second only to Herdwicks for their hardiness, can be identified by a fine set of spiral horns and a black face about a white nose. A Swaledale as a crossing breed, is the mother of such hybrids as the Mule and the Masham.

As you walk, look left to see Ingleborough. The track comes close to a fence. Just before Ghyll Head Road, a narrow lane, take the kissing gate on your right onto a track, which runs beside woodland. Walk the railed duckboards on your left and continue to a stile. At the next stile, walk ahead to the three-

Windermere from Rosthwaite Heights

armed signpost. Continue straight up the slopes to the cairn on Rosthwaite Heights for a panoramic view of the Lakeland mountains, with Windermere below, a very large blue stretch of water.

Return to the three-armed signpost and turn left, then walk ahead in the direction of Rosthwaite farm. At the gate to the dwelling, carry on along the reinforced track to pass the large house on your left and an attractive pond on the right. Ignore the footpath on the right and stroll ahead, with a magnificent view ahead. Follow the track, downhill. Just before the next farm, turn right in front of the last wall before the road.

Go on along the wall to a gate and beyond, with a hedge to the left, climb gently to a gate – a caravan site lies to your right. Follow the walled track to pass in front of the bonny Barker Knott farm. At the road, turn right and, after a hundred yards, take the signposted footpath on the left.

Walk right, as directed, to a gate. Beyond take the upper track, which first continues ahead, then swings left and then right, to a kissing gate. Cross the access track to a cottage and take the footpath opposite. Keep beside the wall on the left, and follow it to pass through a gate. Stride on through two more gates and bear right to pass to the right of Lindeth farm. (Good map reading practice here). Follow the farm track as it swings right and walk on to Lindeth Lane, where you turn right.

Yellowhammer in hawthorn

Once beyond Outmoss, turn left to cross the cattle grid of Low Lindeth. At the second telegraph pole, turn right onto the open fell. Here you might see yellow hammers calling from the top of hawthorns. Continue ahead, keeping parallel with the wall to your right.

At the fence, continue with it on your right and walk to the ladderstile over the long wall descending the fell. Once over, stride ahead up the fell slopes, with a cairn on top of a fell to your left. The way soon becomes a wide, grassy track that leads to a gate to a narrow walled track, where you turn left.

Enjoy this glorious; gently ascending way, which is hedged with broom. Look across the pastures ahead to see the tower of the ruined St Catherine's church ahead (see walk 19), and then join the road. Turn right and after two hundred yards take the pleasing narrow hedged lane on the left, which drops steadily downhill. Ignore the sharp left bend, where it swings away to

Crosthwaite. Walk on downhill along a reinforced track to a gate to the right of a bank barn set in a lovely hollow below the oak-clad Bow Mabble Breast (bank barns explained walk 12).

Climb the grassy track ahead, with the wall to your left. Ascend the gated way and at the brow a grand view of the fells awaits you. Then the track descends steadily to the A5074, where you turn right. Just before the Brown Horse, turn left to visit the church. In spring its churchyard is renowned for its wild daffodils. The grey slate church is dedicated to the Holy Trinity and was consecrated in 1875. It stands on the site of a previous church, possibly 16th century. Return to the main road, turn left and stroll on to rejoin your car.

Bank Farm, Bow Mabble Breast

17. Ill Bell Range

Troutbeck – Yoke – Ill Bell – Froswick – Troutbeck Park farm –
Troutbeck

Start/Finish: Park in the layby, in the side turn that runs close to
Trout Beck, on the north side of Church Bridge (GR 414028).
Troutbeck lies 9 miles from Kendal. The parking area is reached
via the A591 and then the A592.

Type of Walk: This is a challenging 9½-mile walk over high fells
to three summits. It is a grand walk of contrasts which ends with
a gentle stroll through Troutbeck valley, where in summer its one
hedged road is lined with a great variety of wild flowers.

Map: Outdoor Leisure 7, The English Lakes, South Eastern area

---

The Walk

The fells, Yoke, Ill Bell and Froswick form a high-level spine
between the valleys of Kentmere and Troutbeck. Yoke is the
first summit attained on the way from Garburn Pass to High
Street. Then comes the graceful coned top of Ill Bell, linked to
its neighbour on either side by easy ridge walks. Froswick
replicates Ill Bell's shape but is a lesser but delectable top. Blue
Gill slashes the Troutbeck side of Froswick from top to bottom.

From the layby cross the footbridge beside the road bridge
and walk south for 200 yards along the A592. Cross the road to
take the signposted way that climbs steeply – Garburn Road,
the rough track that takes you over the Garburn Pass. It was the
old road from Troutbeck to Kentmere.

Continue on the walled way, from where, after two sharp
turns, you can look down on the Troutbeck valley, and to its
hamlets of Townhead, Townend, The Cragg, High Green and
Longmire Yeat, which nestle against the western hills. Look
upwards, towards the route you will take over the three tops.

Keep on the pitted, boulder-strewn upward way, into the

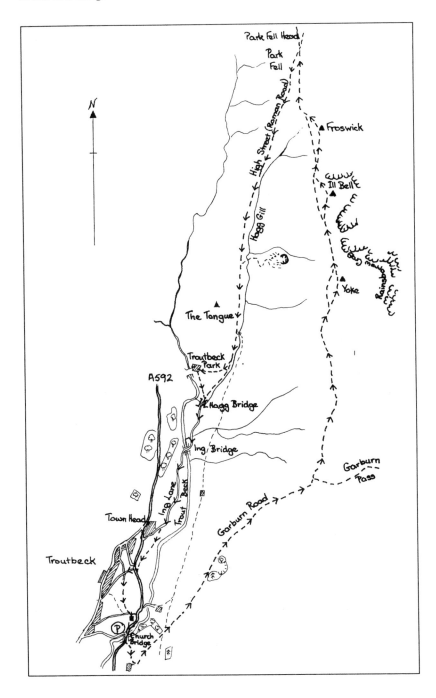

Skylark

territory of skylark
and meadow pipit,
for two miles. Look
for a recent planting
of Norway spruce on
the right and then
pass through a gate
across the track
which has a date
and initials carved
on it. Beyond, at the
corner of the fence,
leave the track to fol-
low the well cairned but indistinct path off left, once the track
to a quarry. After initial wetness the grassy way stretches
upwards. At a large cairn bear off right and go on the cairned
way, gradually coming close to a wall on the right. Continue by
the wall to an easy-to-spot ladderstile which lies about a mile
from Garburn Pass.

Once over, look for the hogg-holes in the sturdy wall. These
allow young sheep, known as hoggs, to pass from one pasture
to another while keeping back larger animals. The holes can be
closed by a large stone.

Beyond the stile the path is indistinct but you soon join a
clear way. Follow the path and head towards a large cairn. You
are now at 600m (2100ft) and at this point you realise that this
is not the summit of Yoke. It lies ahead, and up, 706m (2309ft).
If you wish to avoid the way to the summit, a narrow path
continues ahead, skirting the top. As you go on towards Ill Bell
you have a good view down to Kentmere Reservoir (see walk
18).

The route up to the three well constructed cairns on the
graceful cone-shaped summit 780m (2476ft) is clear. The views
are spectacular, particularly of Windermere. Coming off the top
needs care and a head for heights. Again if it is too windy, or

Summit cairns on Ill Bell

you wish to avoid the steep climb up and down from the peak, you can take a narrow path skirting left of the top.

Stroll the shoulder leading to Froswick. Yet another good path leads to and from the summit 720m (2359ft) and there is one skirting to the left, below the top. Descend from the small peak and continue above Blue Gill. Three hundred yards beyond the ravine, leave the main route, which continues to Thornwaite Crag, and take a narrow grassy path, left, that joins Scot Rake, the path from the Crag. Here you turn left to begin your long descent over Park Fell towards The Tongue, which you see ahead.

As you descend, for nearly a mile, look down to see Hagg Beck snaking through the valley bottom. Beyond a gate, saunter on below the formidable sides of the Froswick and Ill Bell. As you pass a disused quarry, notice the grassy zig-zag incline down which slate was removed. Ignore the National Trust footpath, which goes off left, and go on along the good track.

Follow this as it swings right and walk on to Troutbeck Park farm. Pass left between the buildings and then left in front of the delightful farmhouse.

Beatrix Potter bought this farm in 1923 and did some of her writing here. On bequeathing the farm to the National Trust she insisted that her flock of Herdwick sheep should remain with it. They were probably the ancestors of those you see in the valley pastures about this picturesque corner.

Press on along the lane to cross Hagg Bridge, where the Hagg unites with the Trout. Stride on to cross Ing Bridge, which has stock holes that allow sheep to move to pastures on either side of the road. Proceed to where the lane swings sharp right to Town Head. Here go ahead along a delightful hedged track that

Troutbeck Church and Ill Bell

climbs gently to the A592, which you cross. Walk on along another glorious lane to a signposted track to the church, going off left.

Walk the lovely way, to take a kissing gate on the right, Stroll above the rolling pastures to pass through two more kissing gates to a stile to a track. To visit the church, cross to a white gate and bear left. The church, unusually dedicated to Jesus, is a haven of peace. Enjoy its beautiful east window, designed by William Morris, Maddox Brown and Burne Jones. Its predominant colour is green, rare for a church window, but seeming just right for this charming corner of Troutbeck. Leave the churchyard by its lower lych gate and turn right to rejoin your car.

18. Kentmere

Kentmere village – Kentmere reservoir – Hall Cove –
Kentmere village

Start/Finish: There is parking for a dozen or more cars close to
the Church of St Cuthberts, Kentmere (GR 456041), but it is soon
taken up – so get there early. At the time of writing it had not been
decided whether to provide a bus service from Kendal. If the
answer is yes, you might prefer to "park and ride" to reduce
vehicle pressure on the lovely hamlet, which lies nine miles north
of Kendal. (Bus enquiries 01946 632222).

Type of Walk: This 8-mile walk explores the tranquil, secluded
valley, skirts the Kentmere reservoir and seeks out the source of
the River Kent, which flows through Kendal and gives the town
its name. There are paths and tracks, generally level, for most of
the way. Steady and sometimes wet climbing beyond the reservoir.

Map: OS Outdoor Leisure 7, The English Lakes, South Eastern
area

The Walk

The Kentmere valley remains largely unspoilt because it lies off
the main tourist routes and only one road provides access. The
delightful cement-faced church stands on a small hill. Go inside
to see the 16th century roof beams and enjoy the peaceful plain
interior, refurbished and decorated in the 1990s. Look for the
splendid display of embroidered kneelers which rest, colour-
fully, on the pew ledges.

Walk on beyond the church, from where you have a good
view of Kentmere Hall. Its 14th century pele tower was built for
protection against Scottish marauders. Adjoining the hall is a
16th century farmhouse. The Gilpin family lived here. One
Gilpin, in the 14th century, is reputed to have slain the last wild

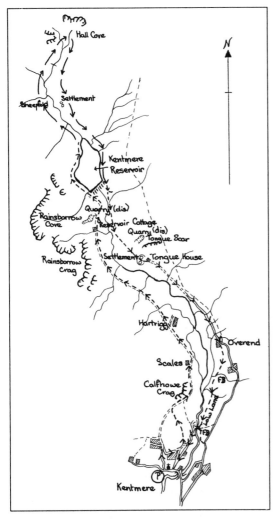

boar in Westmorland. Another, Bernard Gilpin, nearly lost his life for his faith as an ardent protestant but Mary Queen of Scots died and Bernard lived on.

Take the way on the right, signposted Upper Kentmere and Kentmere reservoir, to climb a glorious walled track which passes in front of Head Cottage. In some places the walls are 12 feet high.

Beyond a gate, continue above the village. Just before more dwellings on the track, take another grand walled way (unsignposted), going off on the left. Follow this delightful gated route to rejoin the road, below Raven Crag. Turn right and go along the virtually traffic free road to pass below Calfhowe Crag. Here you might see herons feeding in the marshy area to your right.

Stroll on to pass a small farmhouse, Scales, and look up to see a pleasing waterfall tumbling over the crag above. Proceed along the lane to pass Hartrigg farm, with its small woodland

The waterfall on the Kent

of Scots pine, both on your right. Beyond the signposted gate the way becomes a reinforced track. Then it passes below the formidable Rainsborrow Crag, a flank of Yoke (walk 17). To the right flows the River Kent, its bank lined with alders.

Continue past the buildings set among the disused slate quarry. Go on to the dam of the reservoir. This was constructed in 1845 to catch the fast flowing waters of the Kent and regulate the supply to the many mills along the banks of the river. In more recent times water power has been replaced by other forms of energy.

Towering above to the left is the graceful peak of Ill Bell (walk 17), its rough slopes descending very steeply to the valley floor. Beyond, the way continues as a good path along the same contour above the reservoir. Once beyond it, walk the narrow path to the edge of the beck. Walk beside the hurrying water over the pathless pasture, steadily climbing. Go past attractive waterfalls, the haunt of dippers. Continue upwards past another small fall to a glacial hump in Hall Cove. From here look

Dipper

for several tiny streams draining the steep slopes of High Street before they come together to hurry to the fall. Here the River Kent rises.

Cross the beck and return with it, as it dances downwards, to your right. Keep up the slopes above a sheepfold to see traces of an ancient iron age settlement. Go on towards the reservoir site and join the path that runs above the basin. Step or wade across the Lingmell Beck, which adds its water to the reservoir, and continue to the dam. Here step left across a leat to join a good path continuing on the east side of the beck.

Follow the narrow path as it keeps above the Kent. Skirt the remains of another disused quarry and climb a ladder stile over the next wall. The path continues below Tongue Scar. As you approach the ruins of a barn, look right to see the grassy hollows and banks of Tongue House, another ancient settlement. Here fell ponies graze and come close, hoping to be fed. Pass through gates, keeping to the left of the ruin and then left of a continuing wall.

Stride on along the gated and stiled track. Where the river comes close, enjoy the ancient cobbled packhorse bridge, one of the delights to savour on this walk. Continue until you reach Overend, where you pass through a gate to take the lower waymarked track (right fork) to continue past Overend Cottage and Little Overend. Saunter this delightful way and, on reaching a wider track, Low Lane, bear right. Cross a small clapper bridge, and then another, to follow a public bridleway for Kentmere, proceeding along another fine walled track.

Watch out for the unsignposted stone stepped stile on the right. Beyond, walk ahead to descend to a wooden footbridge. Cross the Kent and continue to a gap stile into another high walled track, where you turn left. Once through the gates of the farm, take the lower track. Ahead you can see Kentmere Tarn, once famous for its diatomite, a clay that was used in face powder, metal polish and coating for paper.

At the track end, cross the road to pass through a kissing gate if you wish to visit the delightful church.

From the church it is a few steps to rejoin your car.

Old drystone bridge, Kentmere

19. Crook

Staveley – Dales Way – Gilpinpark Plantation – Milldam –
St Catherine's Church – Crook – Beckside – Staveley

Start/Finish: Staveley village, which lies 5 miles north-west of
Kendal. It is approached by the A591, which by-passes the
village. Park in the free car park in the centre of the village, beside
the River Gowan (GR 471984).

Type of Walk: An 8½-miler through gentle rolling countryside
about Staveley, partly using the Dales Way. The walk takes you
through no villages, only the smallest of hamlets, and few of
these. Therefore many, perhaps tedious, instructions are given
on this far from tedious walk. Most of the farms of this scattered
rural community are cement rendered, and then whitened, and
are a delight to see.

Map: OS Outdoor Leisure 7, The English Lakes, South Eastern
area

The Walk

Staveley stands at the foot of the Kentmere Valley and was
granted its market charter in 1281. The River Gowan flows
through its centre and unites with the Kent at the south-east
end of the village. These two fast-flowing rivers have provided
water power for corn, smelting, wool, bobbin and fulling mills
over the centuries.

From the car park, turn left. Turn left again, in the direction
of Crook, and pass under the railway bridge and then over the
by-pass. After 200 yards, take the waymarked Dales Way on the
right. Bear left to walk a track to a pasture where, in winter,
children toboggan. Climb steadily right to a kissing gate and,
beyond, go on beside woodland on your left. The way then
continues over open pasture.

At the signpost, before New Hall farm, turn right to walk a

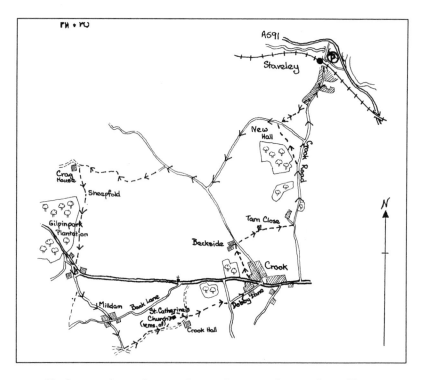

metalled, gated track. To the right stretch gentle rolling pastures, quilted with walls and hedges. If you are walking in spring, listen for the melodious calls of courting curlews.

Walk on along the continuing quiet lane, which gently bears left. Stroll on for nearly a mile. At the T-junction, turn right to walk another narrow lane. Go on for 700 yards and then look left for the Dales Way signpost, where you leave the lane to walk a walled track continuing through pleasing high pastures. After 300 yards take the signposted gate in the wall on the right and carry on with the wall to your left. Follow the clear track as it swings right, away from the wall, and then passes through a gate. Stroll on beside a plantation and, once past, bear right to walk with trees to your right.

Go on, bearing slightly left, following a signpost, to pass through a gate. Stride through gorse to climb a stone stepped stile in the wall to walk a cart track leading towards Crag House farm. Pass through the gate over the track where you leave the Dales Way. Take another gate, immediately to your left, to walk due south.

Head over a large pasture to a stile to the left of a gate. Beyond, keep to the right of a sheepfold. Step over a small beck and bear right, walking either the path, or the parallel track, over the delightful slopes opposite Gilpinpark Plantation. Enjoy this pleasing airy way, passing through two more gates to descend a hedged track. Go quietly, giving yourself time to watch the many small birds that inhabit this sheltered way.

Bullfinch

The track ends at the B5284, which you should cross with care, to take a narrow lane, continuing on. Ignore the footpath on the right and, avoiding all side turns, walk the D-class road through pastures. The way is hedged and here you might catch sight of a pair of bullfinches; sometimes the rich red breast or the white back of the male is seen. Listen for the birds' soft clear calls, which sound like "whib whib".

Cross the small brook, where it flows through a sturdy culverted wall. Continue on past Milldam, which supports coots and swans, to Back Lane, where you turn right. A narrow lane goes off left almost immediately. Follow it for 400 yards, then, where it swings sharp right, before a cattle grid, take a gate to a short track on the left. Proceed beside the continuing wall, ignoring the footpath right, to pass through a gate beyond a tiny stream.

Climb up the pasture ahead, following the telegraph poles, to the end of a wall on your left. Turn left before the wall to take

St Catherine's tower

a narrow gap stile. Beyond stands St Catherine's tower, which was built about 1620. Go through the gate in the wall of the enclosure to see all that is left of the old church, which served the parish of Crook from about 1506 to 1880. After that date the main body of the church had to be demolished because of structural defects, the tower only remaining. Restoration work took place in 1993.

Leave by the gate in the wall, drop down the slope and walk slightly left to pass through a gate to stride a track which leads towards Crook Hall. This is now a farmhouse, built in the 18th century on the site of the manor house. Pass through the next gate and take the single gate on the left. Bear right across the pasture to take a stile in the far right corner. Stride on beside the wall on the right and then go on, when it swings away right, to a ladderstile in the wall ahead. Bear slightly left to descend beside a tree-clad scar to a kissing gate in the lower left corner. Descend slightly right to cross a stile to a lane.

Cross and walk on along Dobby Lane. It was given this name because it was believed to be haunted – so beware. As you near the centre of the scattered village, look left to see part of the old

Crook Mill, now several pleasing houses. This was at one time a fulling mill, with tenter fields on either side.

At the B5284, turn left and climb beside woodland. Take the stiled footpath, signposted Beckside, in the wall on the right. Go ahead over rough pasture and continue climbing a narrow path through gorse, sweetly perfumed when in bloom. Continue to a ladderstile. Beyond, cross the tractor bridge over the beck and head towards the right corner to take a stile to the right of Beckside cottage. Turn right, cross a narrow lane and climb the signposted footpath up the steepish fell slope. Continue over the top, climbing two stiles to walk beside a tarn on your right, just before Tarn Close farm. Stride its access track to Crook Road, where you turn left.

From here it is one and a half miles to Crook. If you find the road too busy, walk for 600 yards and take the footpath on the left, signposted New Hall. Continue across two pastures to turn right onto the Dales Way, walked earlier, to return to Crook Road, just before it crosses the by-pass. Stride left, and then right when you have crossed the River Gowan to rejoin your car.

Old mill, now cottages, Crook

20. Green Quarter

Staveley – Cocklaw Fell – Longsleddale – Green Quarter – Staveley

Start/Finish: Park in the public car park in the centre of Staveley a quiet village, now by-passed by the A591 (GR 471984). It lies 5 miles north-west of Kendal.

Type of Walk: This exhilarating 12-miler takes you over the remote moorland of Cocklaw Fell to look down on the tiny hamlet of Sadgill in Longsleddale. After rain the path over the moor can be wet. It returns you by good paths over Hollow Moor to Green Quarter and then across the pastures to Elf Howe and Staveley.

Map: OS Outdoor Leisure 7, The English Lakes, South Eastern area

The Walk

Leave the village by the narrow road signposted Kentmere. Bear right to cross Barley Bridge, where in the 14th century there was a working corn mill. In 1620 the bridge was the scene of a meeting of "border tenants", farmers who held their land on condition they provided fighting men to defend the border against the Scots.

James I was already king of Scotland when he became king of England in 1603 and he decided to dispossess the tenants. When they opposed him, they were summoned to the Star Chamber, and the meeting at Barley Bridge was to plan their tactics. To conceal the purpose of the meeting they invited the High Constable, saying they wanted him to look at a fault in the bridge. Later they won their case before the Star Chamber and kept their land.

Once over the bridge, bear left to walk the gradually ascending Hall Lane. To the left is a pleasing view of the Kentmere valley. Continue up the lane as it moves out into the pastures

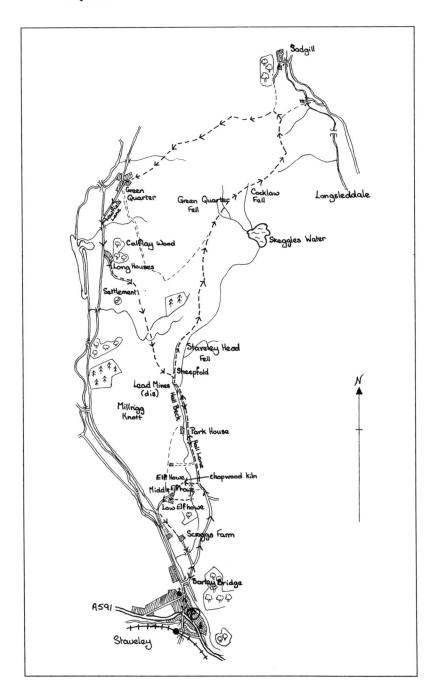

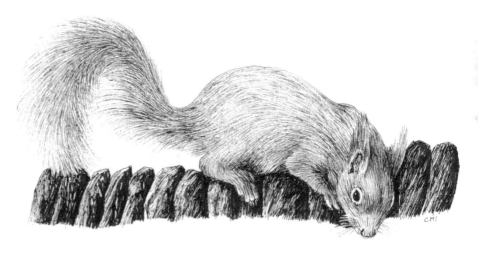

Red squirrel on a wall

below Staveley Head Fell. Here you might see a red squirrel dancing along the wall.

At Park House the tarmacked lane ends and a reinforced track continues. Pass through the gate over the track and continue ahead on the bridleway, passing a sheepfold on your left. Go through the next gate, which is waymarked, and follow a second waymark, directing you right. Proceed along the clear way as it steadily ascends. At a cairn, where the path divides, take the left branch, which continues above a conifer plantation to your left. As you stroll, enjoy the glorious views of the mountains and valleys.

The path brings you to a gate in the top right corner of the huge pasture. To your right the heather covered slope is glorious in August. Follow the path as it bears slightly right across the remote Green Quarter Fell above Kentmere. Under the medieval system of border tenure, the fells in this area were divided into four quarters. Each quarter was sub-divided and the border tenants of each sub-division had to provide a fighting man. The other quarters are Hallow Bank, Wray and Crag.

As you go on, look for the black, long tailed fell ponies feeding

Longsleddale

on the higher slopes. At a gap in the wall, look right to see Skeggles Water, a blue tarn set in an austere hollow. Stride on to take a stile beside a gate from where you can see the tarn almost in its entirety.

Go on the gated way over the lonely Cocklaw Fell and then the trees of Longsleddale come into view. The path, now indistinct, begins to descend steadily to a wall. The gate lies 150 yards from the left corner. Beyond descend parallel with a ruined wall and then follow a grand grassy track as it swings away left with a delightful view of Longsleddale below.

Pass through a gate in the right corner and almost immediately a waymarked gate on the right. Continue in the same direction, keeping beside the wall, now on your left. Cross a dancing stream and take the ladderstile over the wall on your left. Join the track coming from the valley and stroll left, uphill, using a reinforced track. At the top of the slope, look right to see two pretty waterfalls. Ahead take the ladderstile to the left of the gate, to leave the track and join the good stiled path that takes you across the lower slopes of Hollow Moor to Green Quarter.

The track joins a lane opposite a delightful farmhouse with two bank barns, once the old forge. Turn left and walk downhill. At the T-junction, go left to walk Lowfield Lane. From here you have a good view of Kentmere Hall, a fortified farmhouse nestling below Kentmere Park. Look for St Cuthbert's church, standing on a knoll in the middle of the valley, and Kentmere Tarn stretching away towards Staveley.

On joining the valley road, head on left to take the bridleway on the left for Staveley Head. Follow the track right to pass Longhouses, with Calflay Wood behind. Press on along the walled cart track beside deciduous woodland to take the left of two gates. Stride on to the open fell.

Watch out for a row of Scots pine – here the track appears to swing left up the fell, whereas the right of way continues ahead (right) to a waymarked gate, just above the pines. Go on along the gated way. Over the wall on the right is the site of a Romano-British settlement. Beyond the next gate look for the waymark, on a short post, directing you ahead over the pasture, where the track swings right. To your left is the plantation passed, on its far side, earlier in the walk.

Go on over the bracken covered fell. Just before the second gate, a right of way leads right, to the remains of old lead mines (look for spoil heaps), below Millrigg Knott, which you might wish to visit.

To continue the walk, go through the gate and cross left to the far left corner to a gate onto the reinforced track walked earlier. Beyond, turn right and continue past Park House and walk on for 800 yards.

Take the stile, through the wall on the right, signposted footpath to Elf Howe. Just beyond, bear left to the side of a small beck to see an oval-shaped walled enclosure, which is believed to be a kiln for drying chopped wood. Continue over the pasture to climb a stile in the wall. Cross the next pasture to pass through a gate. Beyond, a grassy track leads to a bridge over Hall Beck, just before it descends in dramatic cascades. Climb up the slope to pass through the ruined buildings of Elf Howe to a footpath sign that directs you left through a metal gate.

Descend steadily, with the wall to your left. Pass through a gate and stride across the pasture to pass through another gate. Drop down the slope, left, to a signposted gate onto a lane at Mid Elfhowe. Turn right and walk to the Kentmere Road. Turn left and leave the road immediately by the bridleway on your left, another delightful gated and walled way.

Bear right beyond a barn to walk in front of Scroggs farm and continue along the bridleway to Hall Lane. Turn right to pass through the houses of Staveley to rejoin your car.

Wood drying kiln, Elf Howe

21. Staveley – Burneside

Staveley – Dales Way – River Kent – Cowan Head – Bowston
– Burneside – Braban House – Staveley

Start/Finish: Start from the village of Staveley. Use the small car park on the east bank of the River Gowan, which flows through the centre of the village, a quiet and peaceful corner of Cumbria now that it has been by-passed (GR 471984).

Type of Walk: This is a glorious 7½-mile walk through charming countryside, suitable for all ages. It follows the well signposted Dales Way beside the River Kent to Burneside Hall. It returns over gentle pastures, through delectable woodland and beside the chattering river once again.

Map: OS Outdoor Leisure 7, The English Lakes, South Eastern area

---

The Walk

Turn left out of the car park and left again over the River Gowan, a small feeder of the River Kent. The name Staveley means 'a wood or glade where staves are cut'. The village is the gateway to the upper vale of the Kent. In the past it was a busy village of mills making full use of the water power provided by the River Kent. It is believed that Staveley had two fulling mills in the 12th century. Today it still has several small workshops but it is altogether a different place, with very little industrial noise to disturb its tranquillity.

Continue on to pass under a railway bridge. Just before the next bridge, over the bypass, take a narrow reinforced walled access track on the left, signposted Dales Way. Pass between two dwellings and take the signposted stile through the wall ahead. Turn left and stride to a kissing gate and then a gate. Turn left to pass under another railway bridge and continue to rejoin the road, which you cross. Walk right and go on for 250

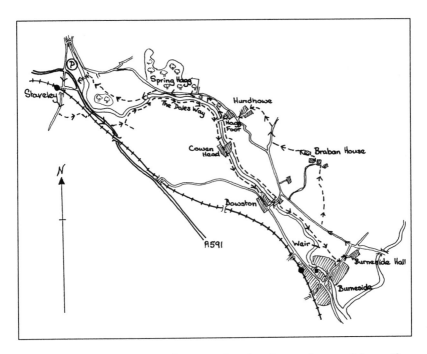

yards, the route of the Dales Way having been changed from the
OS map. A sign directs you to a hedged track on the left.

At a three-armed signpost stride on the Dales Way beside a
wall on the left. Pass through a kissing gate to drop down beside
the hurrying Kent. The river was checked for salmon nests –
known as redds – at the end of 1995, after the summer's drought.
The National Rivers Authority fisheries officers were con-
cerned that a low flow in the river would mean fewer salmon
spawning. But they found the number of redds to be the highest
recorded. A redd is created when the female salmon digs a hole
in the gravel with her tail for the eggs. Her mate then fertilises
them. The female moves upstream slightly to flick gravel on the
eggs to protect them from predators and the fast currents.

Stroll on downstream and begin your dipper count, looking
for a rotund, short-tailed bird with a startlingly white bib. It
perches on rocks round which water swirls. Often all you can
see is a moving patch of white – if it stays still it's litter! The

bird bobs up and down in spasmodic curtsies from which it acquires its name. Look for it where the shallow water hurries over small rocky falls. Here it walks into the water, often using its wings to progress as it seeks for larvae of aquatic insects. It makes its presence known with a shrill 'zit, zit, zit' call.

Pass through a gap in the wall and go on to take ladderstiles into, and then out of, a small copse. From now on the stiled and gated way is well marked and requires no specific directions. Once out of the trees continue on to walk a grassy pasture and then pass left of a derelict barn. Ignore the tractor bridge over the river and go on along the path beside the dancing water. Look for grey wagtails flitting over the water; these slim yellow birds have an undulating flight.

As you near Cowan Head you might see goosanders; the handsome male has a glossy green-black head and is often accompanied by two red-headed ducks with silvery bodies. Cowan Head was once a rag-paper mill and then became derelict but, as this book went to press was being pleasantly refurbished as apartments. It sits astride a large weir which once turned a huge water-wheel. Along this reach of the river look out for kingfishers.

Kingfisher

Stroll on along the continuing lane. Leave it where it swings right and walk on along a track that leads into Bowston. Look for the rockery garden of one of the cottages; it has many model animals among the plants and rocks and a welcoming notice for walkers along the Dales Way. The cottage is one of four in

The bridge at Bowston

Winstanley Row, built in 1880 for mill workers by James Winstanley Cropper, owner of the Cowan and Burneside paper mills. Go on into the village, passing Winstanley Place, where cottages stand on three sides of a green.

Turn left before the post box to cross the sturdy stone arched bridge to take the continuing Dales Way on the far side. Stroll on beside the lovely river, where you might see a heron hunched over the riverbank, waiting patiently for prey. Where the river swings away right, look out for the path going on over a sheep pasture. Pass a large weir and walk on to climb a stile under the shadow of Croppers huge paper mill.

In a few steps pass a metal gate, supporting a large C for Cropper, and then turn left to walk a fenced and hedged path that continues along two sides of the mill. After the last stile and before the stone stile to the road, turn left to walk another narrow fenced track. Look over the wall as you go to see Burneside Hall, a 16th century manor house adjoining a 14th century pele tower built for the defence of Kent dale. It has the remains of an enclosing wall, traces of a moat and an old gatehouse.

At the end of the track pass through a kissing gate onto the main road. Turn left into a hedged lane and stroll on to take a footpath on the right, signposted Braban House. Strike ahead over a large pasture, with a stream to the left, to a gap stile. Go ahead over the next field to pass through a gate. Continue on with a pleasing view of Braban House to the left to pass through a gate onto a track, which lies to the left of a ruin.

Turn left and walk the quiet way. After 200 yards, turn right into a reinforced track before the first building, a cottage. Go on to walk behind outbuildings and then the back of the gracious Braban House to pass through a waymarked gate. Strike left to another waymarked gate and then cross the pasture beyond to join a delightful hedged track, which you walk to the end, at Potter Fell Road.

Stroll right for two hundred yards and take the signposted bridleway, on the left, for Hagg Foot. Continue on along another glorious way which leads into the delectable countryside. Pass through a gate beyond a dwelling on the left. Climb steadily to the three-armed signpost, from where there is a dramatic view into Kentmere.

Follow the directions for Hundhowe, descending steadily another walled track to pass through the farm and onto the road. Turn right to pass the tiny cluster of dwellings at Hagg Foot and take the signposted footpath on the left beyond the last building. Bear left round a tall wall. Pass through two sets of double gates to join a lane dropping down towards the River Kent. Just before the tractor bridge, passed earlier on the other side, take the stile on the right.

This gives entry to the trees of the Woodland Trust, where a friendly notice says that visitors are welcome to walk in its woods. Follow the clear path, deep in oak leaves, and when level with the ruined barn on the opposite bank, look for the narrow left turn. This leads to the side of the river and then onto a footbridge over Hagg Beck. Enjoy the continuing path beside the glorious Kent and as you near the end of the trees bear right along a narrow path to come to the road again.

Walk left, with Spring Hagg wood to your right. Some of the trees show signs of earlier coppicing, reminding you that one of the mills in Staveley made bobbins from the timber. Pass the small sewage works and take the signposted footpath beyond, on the left. Walk the clear path to climb a stone stepped stile.

St Margaret's Tower

Continue ahead as the river loops away to the left. Go on with a wall to the right and climb a ladder-stile. Continue towards woodland, with Staveley Park, white and gracious to the right. At the wall of the woodland, pass through a kissing gate and walk a pleasing track, right. Stride the gated way. Beyond a green metal gate by the barn of the farm, stride diagonally across the pasture in the direction of the bridge to join a track beside the river.

Saunter on to the bridge, which you cross. Another pleasant track takes you into Staveley, passing on the right of what was once a bobbin mill.

At the end of the track stands St Margaret's Tower. This is all that remains of a 14th century chapel built by William de Thweng, who also obtained a market charter for Staveley. Here in the precincts in AD 1620 the rights of border tenant farmers were upheld (see walk 20). In 1864 the church of St James's was dedicated.

Turn right to walk the main street to rejoin your car.

22. Potter Tarn and Gurnal Dubs

Garnett Plain – Garnett Bridge – Docker Nook – Brunt Knott farm – Potter Tarn – Gurnal Dubs – Garnett Bridge – Garnett Plain

Start/Finish: Leave your car in the parking area by the telephone box at Garnett Plain, on the A6, five miles from Kendal (GR 526990).

Type of Walk: This is a lovely roller-coaster 8½-mile walk, generally easy, which keeps beside the River Sprint as it hurries through Longsleddale. It climbs high over the rough col between Potter Fell and Brunt Knott to descend to Over Staveley. It then climbs beside Potter Tarn and the picturesque Gurnal Dubs to drop down the pleasing zig-zags to Garnett Bridge.

Map: OS Outdoor Leisure 7, The English Lakes, South Eastern area

The Walk

Take the signposted stile out of the layby to descend to a stile at the bottom of the steeply sloping field. Turn right and go along the quiet tree-lined lane to the hamlet of Garnett Bridge. This picturesque hamlet lies at the entrance to Longsleddale. Here the River Sprint hurries over its rocky bed and through a tiny gorge, crossed by the delightful bridge, on its way to join the River Kent.

Beyond the bridge take the reinforced track on the right, after passing in front of a cottage called Inglenook. Go through a gate over the track and continue on the bridleway towards Nether House farm, with the Sprint hurrying between its tree-lined banks. Pass through a gateless gap to stride on, with a derelict wall to the left. Climb steadily right, to the next stile in the wall ahead. Stroll through a waymarked gate and continue along a good track.

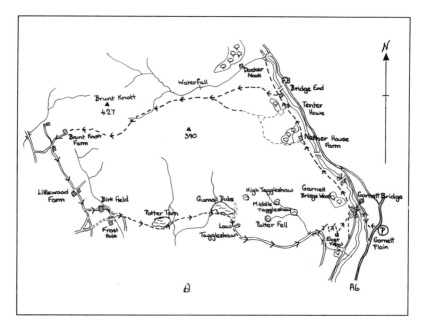

Buzzard soaring

As you walk, watch out for a buzzard circling overhead. It sails gracefully and easily, the flight feathers of its rounded wings splayed out. It fills the air with its high eerie call. Buzzards are often seen over the Lake District, sometimes in pairs, and in summer they are joined by their young so that you might see up to five of these handsome birds on the wing.

On this part of the walk, look for the skilfully placed interlocking stone flags used for fencing. Pass through the next gate onto Nether House farm access road and walk to the right side of the dwelling and outbuildings. To the right lie the steep slopes of Murthwaite Knott and Whiteside Pike. Suddenly you have a wonderful vista ahead of the delightful Longsleddale and, beyond, the towering heights of Harter Fell.

Ignore the left turn by a ruined farm (Tenter Howe) and walk on. Opposite a renovated barn at Bridge End, pass through a gate on the left, signposted Staveley and Kentmere. Bear right across the pasture and walk on. Soon you can see the pleasing white house of Docker Nook, with Kilnstones Wood behind. Below the wood, and out of sight, stands Kilnstones farm. We do not visit it on this walk but from the 17th century it provided hospitality for packhorsemen, drovers and traders who used the route we have walked so far. In the 18th century travellers used this route to avoid paying tolls on the Shap turnpike.

Avoid side turns and go on climbing the good track. Soon the delightful waterfall and cascades in Dockernook gill come into view. Go on, with the gill below to your right.

The track takes you up into the heart of the lonely fells. Soon a glimpse of the ladderstile over the wall ahead encourages you across the slopes. Once beyond, walk ahead for 50 yards and then turn left to follow a narrow path to a stile over a fence. Continue ahead in the same general direction, soon to join a good grassy track over the summit of the col.

Now the way is steadily down and passes a small tarn. Look ahead to see Reston Scar, which overshadows the village of Staveley, and, to the left, Morecambe Bay, silvery in the sunshine. Go through the gate in the fell wall to pass through Brunt Knott farm and join a metalled road. Follow it as it bears left.

At a corrugated barn, where the road swings right, continue ahead in the direction of Littlewood farm. Pass the gated farm and head on to take the left turn to Birk Field. Follow the waymarks to pass in front of the pretty cottage and then bear right beyond the next stile. Keep beside the stream and go on to edge a birch woodland that almost obscures a dwelling named Frost Hole.

Climb left, keeping beside the wall on your right, to a gate onto the fell. Beyond follow the signpost for Potter Tarn, directing you right and then almost immediately left. Ascend steadily to pass through a gap on the right and then a gate on the left. Climb straight up, pausing to enjoy the view of the Langdale Pikes and the Coniston range. Continue ascending, slightly to the right, to see Potter Tarn, now on your left. Climb the stile to the right of the dam and then strike left to walk below the rather intrusive structure, crossing the outflow stream. Continue left to climb another stile in the far left corner.

From the top of the stile, look for the path climbing steeply through the heather to the stile on the skyline, which you take. Beyond this stile a pleasing level track continues through heather to cross the low dam over Gurnal Dubs. Pause here to enjoy the tranquil scene, where on the far side beech, larch, broom, birch and oak crowd a small island. Here you might see a dipper that occasionally nests in a hole between the stones of the dam.

Stride on over the heather, from where grouse call, to join a reinforced track, where you turn right. To the right lies Low Taggleshaw, one of a series of reeded pools. All the pools and tarns were formed by glacial moraine. Gurnal Dubs and Potter

Gurnal Dubs

C. M. Sherwood

Tarn, in the 19th century, came into the possession of James Cropper, the paper maker, who turned them into reservoirs to supply power for his mill at Burneside (see walk 21).

Stride on, with Kendal and Burneside coming into view in the valley below. Pass through the kissing gate and press on along the high-level track, savouring magnificent views of the Howgills and Shap Fells. Continue over Routen Beck and walk on to pass through a signposted kissing gate on the left, at a point where the track turns sharp right. Walk ahead to a waymarked post, keeping the wall to your right. Drop down, slightly left to a waymarked stile and gate. Follow the track bearing left, to another waymark. Here you are directed sharply right to a ladderstile over the wall. Bear left to a stone stepped stile over the wall. Drop down the slope to pass through a gateless gap and then down again, before the first house of Garnett Bridge, which has many conifers in its garden. Go to a signposted stile (easy-to-miss) to the road. Turn left and continue to cross Garnett Bridge and walk right. Climb the narrow lane until you reach the signposted stile (the second signpost) to climb the steep pasture to Garnett Plain.

Garnett Bridge

23. Shipman Knotts and Kentmere Pike

Sadgill Bridge, Longsleddale – Shipman Knotts – Kentmere
Pike – Harter Fell – Gatescarth Pass – Sadgill Bridge

Start/Finish: The tarmacked road through Longsleddale ends at
the hamlet of Sadgill. Here a pleasing arched bridge spans the
sweetly chattering Sprint river. There is parking by the bridge for
several cars(GR 483057). Farm vehicles make frequent use of
the road end, the bridge and the continuing quarry track and good
access must be left for these. Sadgill lies 10 miles from Kendal.

Type of Walk: There is a climb right at the start of this 7½-mile
walk and there is more as you go on to ascend to Shipman Knotts.
But once you reach the summit of Kentmere Pike – an extensive
area of moorland – the views make the effort all worth while. From
then on the way is nearly always down, with even more spectacular views to make this a glorious walk. There are clear paths
to follow but choose a good day.

Map: OS Outdoor Leisure 7, The English Lakes, South Eastern
area

The Walk

Four miles from Kendal, along the A6 road to Shap, stands the
sign for Longsleddale. The narrow lane drops down to the
charming hamlet of Garnett Bridge and then continues for six
miles through the quiet valley. The lane has few passing places
and the lush vegetation, encroaching on the tarmac, makes it
seem even narrower. Only passengers enjoy this beautiful
drive.

During much of the summer the hedgerow vegetation is a riot
of colour. Woody cranesbill, bloody cranesbill, blinks, red
campion, bistort and herb robert provide the reds and pinks;
the white of ransoms, cow parsley and sweet cicely accentuate

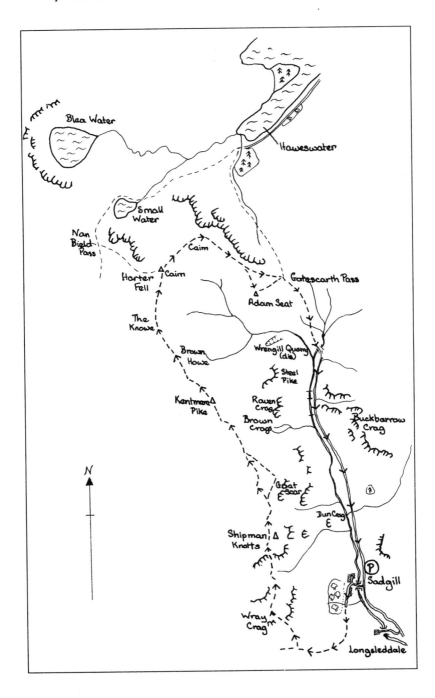

Redstart

the blue of viper's bugloss, bugle and bluebell; and dandelion, buttercup and touch-me-nots add a bright splash of yellow.

The narrow road ends at Sadgill, a tiny hamlet of two or three cottages with pretty gardens. Boulders heavily laden with moss litter the floor of Sadgill Wood and each year redstarts nest close to the footpath.

Cross the bridge and follow the track as it bears left through a gate and then right before the next dwelling. Listen for nuthatch, redstart, great tit, willow warbler and chiff chaff as you pass through the trees. At the signpost, go through the gate to continue on a public by way, arrowed in red. Ascend the rough track to pass through the next gate. Beyond, turn right to begin the climb to Kentmere Pike. The path, always clear, soon comes beside a wall on your right with which you remain for almost all of the walk. The steepish way passes through innumerable rocky outcrops, keeping to the right of Wray Crag.

The summit of Shipman Knotts lies over the wall. It consists of three rocky knolls, the highest – the middle one – 587m. Look back frequently as you climb to enjoy the magnificent views.

Continue to a ladderstile in the wall ahead. Bear right here to visit the cairn on Goat Scar (626m) for a magnificent view, in good weather, over Longsleddale far below. Then go on beside the familiar wall to reach the summit of Kentmere Pike,

Haweswater from Harter Fell

where there is a small cairn. Over the wall, reached by a stepped stile, stands the trig. point. Pause by the cairn and look west to see the tops of Yoke, Ill Bell and Froswick (see walk 17), a ridge parallel to the one you are walking.

Go on from the summit, with the wall to your right. The way continues down and then inexorably up until you reach the cairn on Harter Fell. As you walk, look for Nan Bield Pass, just below on your left. With care walk ahead to see two lovely tarns set in rock-girt hollows, Small Water and Blea Water. Small Water lies in a corrie and beside it ran an ancient packhorse route taking travellers from Kentmere to Mardale, using Nan Bield Pass. Blea Water also sits in a corrie and is reputed to be over 64m deep.

Return to the cairn and follow the fence right (east) and go over the fell top. As you proceed more and more of Haweswater

Waterfalls in Cleft Ghyll

comes into view, providing a pleasant vista. Where the fence swings right again (south east), follow it. Look left to see the track over Gatescarth Pass coming up from the reservoir. Here you may wish to continue by the fence to Adam Seat, with its boundary stone. Or you may prefer to descend the wide rough track that joins the pass at a gate. The fence from Adam Seat comes in here, too.

Turn right and begin the rocky descent into Longsleddale. To the left stretches wild and lonely Mosedale and to the right, Wrengill. Good slate was quarried in the gill, and during the 1939-45 war the work was done by Italian prisoners of war. There is no right of way into the quarries, which are dangerous, but pause on the road to enjoy the glorious waterfalls.

Continue descending the steep zig-zags of the splendidly reinforced quarry road. The track then descends more gently close to the River Sprint, which hurries through Cleft Ghyll in a series of dramatic waterfalls. Look for a tawny owl here and a pair of ring ousels. Beyond, to the right, tower Steel Pike, Raven Crag and Brown Crags. You can also see Goat Scar where you stood earlier.

Follow the track along the valley bottom. It is wide enough for one field only on either side of the river. Pass below Buck-barrow Crag on the left. Go on until you reach Sadgill to rejoin your car.

24. Shap Wells

Shap summit – Spa well – Railway summit – Granite works –
Wasdale Old Bridge – Shap summit

Start/Finish: Long layby on west side of A6, Shap summit (GR
553067). A small yellow building lies just beyond the layby, 10
miles north of Kendal. The A6 is a mere shadow of what it was
in the days before the construction of the M6.

Type of Walk: A good 7-mile walk over high moorland by quiet
tracks and footpaths to Shap Wells, once a spa hotel. Then on
past the summit of the London to Glasgow railway, returning over
the old turnpike road. Go when the slopes are a blaze of purple
heather and the air is full of sweet perfume. For much of this walk
there is little shelter. Warm and water-proof clothing needed.
Walking boots advisable. Turn back if mist descends.

Map: OS Outdoor Leisure 7, The English Lakes, South Eastern
area

The Walk

From the layby, cross the road and walk along (north) a short
distance to take a signposted, stiled and gated bridleway on

Coal tit

your right. Stride the solidly reinforced track, which runs below
Packhorse Hill. Pass through the
gate at the east corner of a large
plantation of conifers. Away to
the right stretch the heather
slopes of Birkbeck Fells Com-
mon. Descend the track.

As you go listen for the calls of
goldcrests, coal tits and wrens in
the firs. Look through the trees to
see the Pink Granite quarry on
Long Fell.

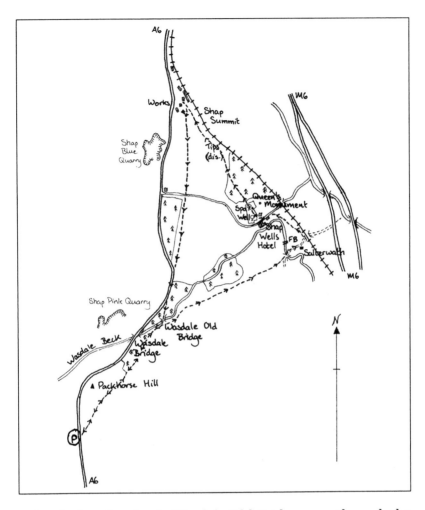

Just before the sturdy Wasdale Old Bridge, pass through the gate on the right and stride the clear grassy track. To your left flows the Wasdale Beck and beyond stretch more conifers. Follow the track as it swings slightly right and then on in the same direction, until you reach the corner of a curving wall on your left. Stroll beside the wall as it curves to the right. Continue downhill, beside a small stream, with the wall always to your left. Join the track to Stonygill, where you turn left, passing through a gate.

Cross the tractor bridge over Birk Beck, where yellow balsam flowers in summer. Look left to see, off the right of way, a pleasing arched footbridge. Go on along the track to walk to the left of Salterwath farm. Follow the track as it swings left. Just before the railway bridge, bear left to walk the rough pasture and after 100 yards bear diagonally left across an area of rush, dropping to a gate half-way along the boundary wall.

Pass through a gate and walk straight ahead to cross the beck on a clapper bridge. Go on to the access track to Shap Wells hotel, where you turn left. Beyond the first house, on the right, a kissing gate gives access to a track climbing uphill to a monument. This commemorates the accession to the throne of Queen Victoria on 20 June, 1837.

Return to the track and continue to the hotel. Walk across the

car park to take a grassy track to the right of a small building. This now provides hotel accommodation but once was the bath-house where visitors bathed in what was considered the health-giving water. Continue up the grassy track beside a lively beck dancing through delightful deciduous woodland. This leads to the Spa well.

The Spa Well

The well was supplied by a spring containing calcium chloride, sodium chloride and magnesium sulphate. People flocked to drink and to bathe in its water.

Where the path divides take the lower path to visit a charming waterfall. Leave this pleasing corner by walking uphill to pass through a gap in the wall, on your left. Turn right to walk to a stile into a ride through sitka spruce. Watch your step here because the furrows, dug when the trees were planted, cross the path and trip the unwary. Step across the drainage dyke beside a wide forest ride which you cross to continue through more serried ranks of trees.

At the edge of the trees, turn right, ignoring the stile ahead, to pass through a gate now on your left. Once through, turn right and follow the wall beside more trees and then on to the side of the railway. Walk left beside it. Its banks are a mass of heather, with willow and aspen lining the top. Go on to pass

Shap Granite Works

through a gate and then to look down on two attractive cottages. These were once railway workers' homes. Just beyond is a board which says that this is Shap summit, 916 ft above sea level.

At this point, strike left across the moorland to the side of the huge granite works. Turn left and walk the wide grassy way of the old turnpike road. As you go you have a ringside view of the various activities taking place as the granite is fashioned.

Pass through a waymarked gate and saunter on. The right of way passes through a sheepfold, crosses the access track to the hotel and continues over Wasdale Foot. Continue to the side of the A6. Walk on for less than a quarter-of-a-mile, using the wide grassy area beside the road. Then drop down left along a reinforced track which is another remnant of the old road, to a gate into conifers. This leads to Wasdale Old Bridge, which you cross. Continue steadily ahead to the gate passed through almost at the start of the walk. Follow the track to the A6, where you turn left to rejoin your car.

25. Otter Bank and Whinfell Tarn

Otter Bank – Selside – Whinfell Tarn – Patton Bridge – Dales Way – Garnett Folds – Otter Bank

Start/Finish: Layby, part of the old highway on the right (east) side of the A6, 3 miles from Kendal (GR 532972).

Type of Walk: This lovely, easy-to-walk route passes through the hilly area of Selside, where farms and houses are surrounded by green pastures bounded by stone walls. The 7-mile walk visits the village church, comes beside Whinfell Tarn and joins a delightful stretch of the Dales Way for the return stroll. Kendalians are fortunate to have such glorious countryside so close to the town.

Map: OS Outdoor Leisure 7, The English Lakes, South Eastern area

---

The Walk

From the layby walk the narrow hedged lane uphill, ignoring the footpath on the right. Where the lane swings right, continue on along a grassy track, Dry Lane, which climbs steadily through quiet pastures. In late spring the hedgerows are a riot of wild flowers, the fields resound to the calls of curlews and each tree seems to have its own migrant, establishing its territory with loud song.

As you go, enjoy the grand views of Whinfell, Kentmere Pike and the Ill Bell range. At the road, turn left and pass through an unsign-

Curlew displaying

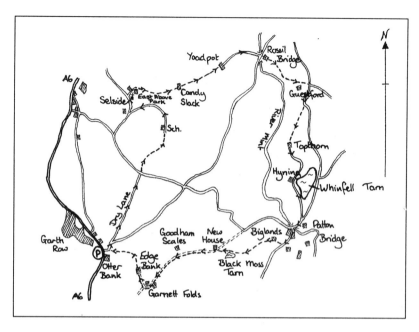

posted gate on the right side of the road. Walk the continuing gated track, through the undulating pastures, towards the roof of a building, nestling in a hollow ahead. The building is Selside primary school, which you pass on the right.

At the lane, turn left and follow it through a bluebell copse and then unfenced pasture. Look right for a pleasing view of St Thomas's church and then stroll on the winding lane to visit it. The church surrounded by yews, looks down on Selside Hall, a fine Elizabethan farmhouse. In the 14th century it was a pele tower. Away to the west is Watchgate Water Treatment Plant, tucked away on the Roman Road. The plant draws water from Windermere, Thirlmere, Haweswater and Ullswater, supplying towns from Barrow to Manchester.

Go on along the lane from the church to take a red metal gate on the right. Walk to the left of East Above Park, and continue along a gated walled track. Go on to cross a small brook, on your left, and follow it upstream a short way before swinging across to the top right corner to a stone stepped stile.

St Thomas's church

Once over, ignore the ladderstile on your left and head across the corner of the pasture towards Candy Slack farm, crossing an unusual stile over an old hedge and wall. Stride ahead to another stile and walk to the left side of the farmhouse to pass through a gate to a reinforced track. Beyond a gateless gap, stroll on to walk beside the wall on your left to cut across the corner to a stile in the wall ahead. Stride on, with the wall to your left. Then, when the chimney pots of Yoadpot come into view, swing away right, from the wall, to pass through a gate, left of the dwelling.

Stroll on and bear right to join the farm's access track. Follow it as it veers right and comes to a road, which you cross. Cross also, ahead, the pleasing old stone bridge over the River Mint. Turn right to pass through a gate. Turn left to walk beside the hedge on your left and then to a ladderstile half-way along the fence ahead. Go towards the river and at the ford leave it to bear left to a gate. Pass through the next gate and go on to pass through the farmyard of Guestford and on along the access track.

At the road, turn right and, where it makes a very sharp left turn, look for the easy-to-miss stile on the right in the corner of

Whinfell Tarn

the wall. Go ahead over a pasture to a stile in the wall, now on your left. Stride on to a gate to a track to Topthorn farm. Pass between the dwellings and outbuildings and bear left to walk the access track. And then Whinfell Tarn lies to your left.

The waters of the tarn are held by glacial debris. Around its reedy edge stretches the good farmland of Hyning and The Borrans. These two face each other across the blue waters of the tarn. Look for coot, moorhen, mallard, swans and geese.

Continue along the reinforced track and then the road as it swings left to pass Hyning farm, from where there is a good view of Whinfell Beacon. Here, fires were lit, warning of marauding Scots. It was not one of the highest hills to be chosen for beacons but the warning flames could be seen clearly from the low-lying land to the west and south, and in particular from Kendal.

Pass through a copse and continue to a T-junction. Turn right to cross Patton Bridge, over the River Mint, and continue uphill beyond. Take the signposted right turn, to join the Dales Way, passing in front of a house named Biglands. Continue on the clearly waymarked path to come to the side of Black Moss tarn, which lies in high fields above the River Mint.

Here the path turns right and then swings left over a small hill with a pylon. Go on in front of New House and follow the sunken track towards Goodham Scales. The way continues as a reinforced track and then a metalled road.

Where the road swings sharp left, pass through a gate ahead, with The Dales Way faintly painted in white. Drop down the steep track to pass through Garnett Folds and on to take the path on the right, signposted Otter Bank. Climb the access track, which is lined with bistort in early summer, to dwellings at Edge Bank. Go through a gate to the left and pass under the overhead power lines to take an ornate metal gate in the far left wall.

Continue ahead to another unusual footbridge and stile on the right (easy-to-miss). Walk ahead from the footbridge, with the wall to your left, and continue through another stile. Go on to another narrow stile to the left of the gate – the signposted stile ignored at the start of the walk.

WALKING LAKELAND TRACKWAYS: the Eastern Lakes

Mike Cresswell

This is the companion volume to Mike's "Walking Peakland Trackways". The walks trace the historical significance of the paths, tracks and minor roads that cross the Lake District. They include: Roman Roads such as High Street and Kirkstone Pass; Mediaeval and Trade Routes – the Corpse Road across Wasdale Head and the Drovers' Road at Muncaster; Turnpikes – from Shap to Kendal and Ambleside to Grasmere. In all, 24 well-planned routes that bring history vividly to life. Distances range from 6 to 16 miles.

£7.95

TEASHOP WALKS IN THE LAKE DISTRICT

What a great idea! Jean Patefield has selected a super range of walks across the entire Lake District and has combined them with some superb teashops. The walks are all quite short and are perfect for family outings. Each walk has a clear sketch map, interesting photographs and snippets of information about what to look for along the walk – while you're looking forward to scones with strawberry jam!

£6.95

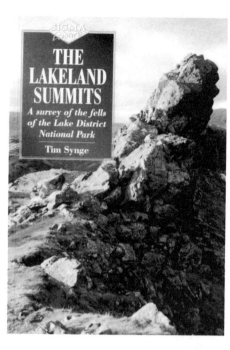

THE LAKELAND SUMMITS: a survey of the fells of the Lake District National Park

Tim Synge

"A really workmanlike job"
MANCHESTER EVENING NEWS

£7.95

FULL DAYS ON THE LAKELAND FELLS: 25 challenging walks in the Lake District

Adrian Dixon

£7.95

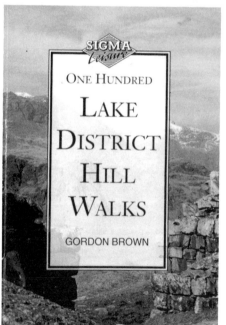

100 LAKE DISTRICT HILL WALKS

Gordon Brown

"A useful addition to any walker's library" WEST CUMBERLAND GAZETTE.

£7.95

LAKELAND WALKING: on the level

Norman Buckley

"A good spread of walks" RAMBLING TODAY.

£6.95

Mostly Downhill

Leisurely walks in the Lake District

SIGMA *leisure* **Alan Pears**

MOSTLY DOWNHILL: Leisurely Walks in the Lake District

Alan Pears

"Perfect companion; thoroughly recommended" MENCAP NEWS.

£6.95

LAKELAND ROCKY RAMBLES: Geology beneath your feet

Bryan Lynas; Foreword by Chris Bonington

"Refreshing ... Ambitious ... Informative ... Inspiring" NEW SCIENTIST.

£9.95

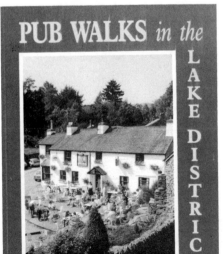

PUB WALKS in the LAKE DISTRICT

Neil Coates SIGMA *leisure*

PUB WALKS IN THE LAKE DISTRICT

Neil Coates

£6.95

CYCLING IN THE LAKE DISTRICT

John Wood

£7.95